Music in American Life

*A list of books in the series Music in American Life
appears at the end of this volume.*

"Happy in the Service of the Lord"

"Happy in the Service of the Lord"

Afro-American Gospel Quartets in Memphis

Kip Lornell

University of Illinois Press
Urbana and Chicago

This book is printed on acid-free paper.

Library of Congress Cataloging-in-Publication Data

Lornell, Kip, 1953-
    "Happy in the service of the Lord".

    (Music in American Life)
    Bibliography: p.
    Includes index.
    1. Gospel music—Tennessee—Memphis—History and
criticism. I. Title. II. Series.
    ML3187.L67   1988   783.7'09768'19   87-35688
    ISBN 0-252-01523-1 (alk. paper)

Contents

Acknowledgments

Several years of research, thought, and revising have gone into this book. Although I take ultimate responsibility for the final product, many people contributed to the project in diverse ways. I need, above all, to thank the quartet singers themselves for their untiring cooperation, patience, and interest in my work. In this regard, Elijah Ruffin, Mrs. Clara Anderson, George Rooks, and Earl Malone provided me with the most information. But there are several dozen other members of the Memphis quartet community who selflessly answered questions, loaned their invaluable photographs to be copied, and provided me with insights.

The selfless generosity of my fellow gospel quartet researchers cannot go unnoted. Lynn Abbott helped with general information, photographs, material about New Orleans quartets, and background data from various newspapers, including the *Louisiana Weekly.* Ray Funk supplied a number of photographs, numerous suggestions, newspaper clippings, and encouragement. Doug Seroff provided many critical, insightful comments at various points, helped me locate photographs, and unselfishly shared information and interviews. Their altruistic assistance helped to make this book a reality.

Three scholars at Memphis State University, David Evans, Ted Mealor, and Dick Raichelson, deserve recognition for their help in developing early drafts of this manuscript. David's thoughtful suggestions shaped the entire manuscript, while Ted encouraged my interest in the geography of music and Dick assisted me in looking at the quartet community. Riki Saltzman requires special notice for her love and moral support, as well as her help and perceptive suggestions in proofreading and revising this manuscript from its genesis.

Val Hicks pointed me toward information about barbershop quartets, and Jack Hurley generously copied many of the photographs that appear in this book. Bill Daniels provided me with invaluable, then unpublished, postwar discographical information for a number of Memphis groups. I also appreciate the efforts of the three anonymous scholars who carefully read prepublication drafts of this manuscript for the University of Illinois Press and who suggested many subtle improvements.

Special thanks also to the National Endowment for the Arts/Folk Arts and the Wenner-Gren Foundation for Anthropological Research for supporting my research and documentation of Memphis quartets while I was a doctoral candidate.

The staff of the Blue Ridge Institute of Ferrum College, especially Roddy Moore, must be cited for allowing me the extreme flexibility that I required to finish this book. Judy McCulloh recognized the promise of this project from its inception and encouraged me through several drafts, while Terry Sears patiently copyedited the final manuscript. The ongoing, selfless support of my parents, Wallace and Betty Jane Lornell, was also critical to the completion of both my education and this book. Each of these people believed in me and in what I could do.

"Happy in the Service of the Lord" is dedicated to Don Lassonde and Georgia Lundquist, both of whom died too young, and also to James Darling and the other Memphis quartet singers who did not live long enough to see their good works documented in print.

"An American in Paris"

The sun was shining brightly, forcing me to squint as I walked along. The glare reflecting from the buildings and the pavement amplified the heat of the brilliant, clear July morning. Children abounded and several older women strolled just ahead of me. I was in a totally foreign section of the city, though my directions suggested that only a five-minute walk lay ahead of me.

My primary landmark was a small store on the right, across the street from a pharmacy and a brightly trimmed florist shop. My pace quickened slightly after I glanced at a clock and noticed that I was a few minutes late. But no one else seemed to be in a hurry, so I relaxed and enjoyed the lovely day. Soon I spotted my destination: a compact, beige, two-story house with a small garden in front.

The front door was ajar, and Mrs. Wilson quickly emerged from the rear of the house. She greeted me warmly and asked me to sit down. For nearly two hours we talked about her husband, Orlandus Wilson, and his group, the Golden Gate Quartet, and watched a stirring videotape of several performances of the group that had been excerpted from two commercially released films and recent concerts. Mrs. Wilson also showed me a large scrapbook filled with vintage photographs, press releases, and clippings. Just the type of relaxed, informal visit researchers dream about.

All too quickly my time was up. As I left the house I turned and consulted my notebook to make certain that I had written down the correct address, so I could write to Mrs. Wilson to thank her and remind her to send me five photographs. Yes, the address was correct: 44, rue des Cervantes. It was then that I realized that this quiet, well-maintained neighborhood was really the only touristless part of Paris I had visited! With that pleasant thought I turned and walked back to the metro to catch the next train to the Marmottan.

That I was exploring the history of Afro-American gospel quartet singing in Paris during the summer of 1984 is not as preposterous as it may seem. The Golden Gate Quartet, originally from the Virginia Tidewater and one of the most popular and influential groups of the 1940s, had left the United States in the middle 1950s. Since the flamboyant, heady days of the 1920s, black American musicians as diversely talented as "Champion" Jack Dupree, Josephine Baker, Louisiana Red, "Bricktop," Slide Hampton, Art Farmer, Sugar Blue, Dexter Gordon, and Kenny "Klook" Clarke, have moved to Europe in search of wider acceptance of their artistry, greater financial rewards, and some relief from racism.

Because so many black American performers have expatriated themselves, a healthy interest in country blues, bebop, and gospel shouters among Europeans is hardly surprising. This interest has had a direct impact on an increasingly international popular and jazz music scene. European musicians like Eric Clapton, John Mayall, Mick Fleetwood, Stephane Grapelli, Joe Zawinual, and Neils Henning Orstead Pederson spent their formative years listening to and learning from the American masters. Now these and other Europeans have had a major influence on popular music and jazz in the United States.

In addition to a direct, lively interest in performing Afro-American music, Europeans were among the field's pioneering scholars. Some of the earliest critical writing about jazz, for example, comes from France. Perhaps the most notable example is Hughes Panassie's *Real Jazz* (1941). Even today, Europeans publish many specialized journals and operate dozens of small record companies devoted to black American music. Several of the finest original-disc collections of American black music from the 1920s, 1930s, and 1940s belong to private European collectors like *Playboy* cartoonist Francis Smith.

This is not to suggest that black American music has been entirely ignored within the United States. In the 1920s and 1930s

Alan Lomax, Winthrop Sargeant, Guy Johnson, John Hammond, and a few others began digging into the lode of music that surrounded them. Since then there have been scores of books and thousands of articles published on Afro-American music. Tens of thousands of commercial recordings covering a wide variety of black American music have been issued in this country over the same fifty-year span.

Despite this intensive research, no one has ever written a truly comprehensive study of black gospel music in America, primarily because religious music generally receives less attention than jazz, blues, or popular music. Only a few writers have tackled the complex, fecund field of Afro-American religious music, though many research topics remain virtually untouched.[1] Certainly quartet singing is one of the most neglected and important forms, as Portia Maultsby points out: "Quartet arrangements of religious and secular songs have been the most popular style of group singing since the beginning of the twentieth century. The Black quartet tradition, and particularly the jubilee group, has had a major influence on the evolution of American music—folk and popular song."[2]

Because so few scholars have examined black American religious music, and quartets in particular,[3] two very basic terms require clarification. The first is *gospel,* a word with many meanings for different people. Black singers occasionally use it when referring to any type of religious music, regardless of the music's age or origin. For these singers the phrases "gospel music" and "religious music" are interchangeable. Older singers, by contrast, more often divide religious music into categories such as hymns, spirituals, anthems, and jubilees. These veterans grew up in a time when "gospel" apparently referred to only one of several types of religious music.

There are also specific formal definitions that add to our understanding of this multifaceted term. In describing the gospel songs of the 1970s, musicologist Horace Boyer writes that this music is "rhythmically distinguished by syncopation, a driving beat, and divisions and sub-divisions of the beat [that feature much] improvisation and highly embellished performances."[4] Pearl Williams-Jones observes that this music contains "contemporary harmonies over embellished lines [that] use a large variety of forms among which are verse-chords, ballads, theme and variations, three-line blues structures, call-and-response chants, strophic, modified strophic and through composed structures."[5]

These technically accurate descriptions complement folklorist David Evans's three cultural criteria "of gospel music in respect to style and social role." Evans correctly asserts that this "music serves as entertainment as well as a religious experience . . . [and] tends to be innovative in both content and style." In concord with the older singers' perspectives, he also points out that gospel "can incorporate all types of religious music."[6] To Evans's description I would add the following observations based on my own research. First, gospel music is transmitted in small group situations through oral means and to larger audiences by way of the mass media. Second, certain elements of gospel music—repertoires and special vocal techniques—are sometimes found in both black and white traditions. Finally, "black gospel" refers to an innovative, popular style of religious music whose songs can be traced to a single composer, such as Thomas A. Dorsey, Cleavant Derricks, or Memphians W. Herbert Brewster and Lucie E. Campbell.

The other major term requiring clarification, *quartet,* also enjoys varied usages. The *New Grove Dictionary of Music and Musicians* defines it as "any composition for four voices or instruments"[7]—a definition that may be appropriate for singers and instrumental music using notated scores but that does not always apply to vernacular American music. For Afro-American religious singers, this definition is not entirely appropriate. Black religious quartets have generally stressed four-part harmony—usually bass, baritone, tenor, and alto—but use between four and six voices, one of which is frequently assigned to a lead singer who improvises his or her part. When more than four voices are singing harmony, some members either temporarily drop out or "double up" on a single part. Gospel quartets perform either a cappella or with minimal instrumental accompaniment, usually some combination of guitar, bass, keyboards, or percussion.

Although definitions related to black American gospel music are still being formulated and clarified, the cultural significance of this music is beyond doubt. What began as a grassroots movement during the first two decades of the twentieth century has become a popular form of music that is performed weekly at thousands of

churches across the country, is available on scores of local and national record labels, and can be heard on regularly scheduled radio
broadcasts. Afro-American gospel music is currently performed in
many genres, such as soloists, choirs, and quartets, each of which
enjoys its own stars, performance style, and unique history.[8]

"Happy in the Service of the Lord" is the first book to examine
in-depth the development and importance of black American religious quartet singing. Specifically, I describe the musical culture of
black gospel quartets in Memphis, Tennessee, from the late 1920s
through the early 1980s. My interest in Memphis quartets encompasses several disciplines and is informed by perspectives from
history, musicology, geography, anthropology, folklore, and sociology. Chapter 1 traces the origin and development of black religious quartet singing in the United States, while the second chapter examines the evolution of this tradition in Memphis. The next
chapter covers geographical and spatial aspects of Memphis quartet singing, particularly in terms of cultural ecology, migration, and
networks. Chapter 4 analyzes and describes the complex, multi-
layered relationships within a special quartet community, empha-
sizing the social organization, quartet training, and performance
contexts. The final chapter probes the symbiotic relationships
among the mass media, popular culture, and black quartets.

The great majority of the information and basic data contained
in this book comes from my fieldwork and research in Memphis
beginning in the fall of 1979. Over a four-year period I spoke with
dozens of active or former quartet singers, eventually selecting
about three dozen for taped interviews. Doug Seroff, a fellow re-
searcher living near Nashville, provided me with several other important interviews and vital leads.

As I gradually became more immersed in this special world, the
complexities of this musical genre became more apparent. Trac-
ing group histories and their often myriad changes in personnel
proved particularly challenging and required great care and patience. The fact that some quartets changed names without altering personnel, while other singers performed with half a dozen
groups during their careers, further obscured the genealogical relationships among groups.

Simply dealing with this many individuals, many of whom moved within very constricted circles, provided another interesting puzzle. I gradually learned who was still speaking with whom, why certain people changed group alliances so often, how specific people rose to positions of prominence within this community, and a whole range of other related personal interactions that affected the dynamics of Memphis quartets. I had to untangle not only the threads of years of personal relationships but also the language of the quartet culture. What, for example, was a "trainer" and how did he work with singers? For that matter, what did "unions" have to do with this music? Several years passed before I was able to master this new lexicon, much of which I suspect is unique to black culture.

In addition to numerous informal conversations and formal interviews, I frequently observed quartet singing in its performance contexts. Occasionally I went to the local churches where the groups sang. These visits proved invaluable for they demonstrated that quartet singing is as much a performance as a musical event. I very rarely attended church programs that featured modern groups, choirs, or choruses in addition to quartets because these ensembles were so often accompanied by uncomfortably loud, electronic instruments; other groups were composed of novices in need of practice and polishing.

I found the quartet rehearsals much more interesting and rewarding than the actual programs. They were less chaotic, more informal, and often featured very inspired singing. I was able to stop the rehearsals to ask questions about musical aesthetics, song arrangements, and how songs are harmonized or arrangements altered. When the singers got together, they often remembered a story or some long-forgotten incident, and sometimes my prompting uncovered interesting songs rarely performed anymore. These weekly rehearsals quickly proved invaluable and I attended many of them between 1979 and 1983.

Visual images, particularly older photographs, provided yet another rewarding avenue for research and information. I located approximately seventy-five different images, including posters, handbills, programs, and still photographs, which provide a visual portrait of quartets from the late 1930s through the early 1980s. These images proved especially useful because they often reminded people of other interesting quartet singers or stories long forgotten. Photos also tell us something more about the singers themselves: how they dressed for a performance, for instance. A representative sample of these photographs and related printed material was assembled for a fall 1982 exhibition at Memphis State University and in the Gaston Park branch of the Memphis–Shelby County Public Library and Information Center.

Another valuable source of primary data were the commercial recordings by Memphis gospel quartets, which began in the late 1920s and continued sporadically for about thirty years. This phenomenon is discussed in several of the chapters and a comprehensive discography is provided in Appendix II. It is noteworthy that playing taped copies of these recordings triggered the memories of musicians who were refreshed by the sounds of singing unheard for so long. While the discography itself contains new, factual information, the conversations with singers moved by these aural documents were equally illuminating.

I also recorded some of the Memphis quartets that were active during the period of my research. The results are professional-quality sound documents of six groups, recorded in Memphis State University's Commercial Music Studio: two 45-rpm records—High Water 419 by the Harmonizers, "Trampin'" and "I'll Be Satisfied," and High Water 420 by the Gospel Writers, "Oh, My Lordy Lord" and "Blind Bartamus"—and a long-playing album, *Happy in the Service of the Lord: Memphis Gospel Quartet Heritage—The 1980s* (High Water 1002). High Water released the album and its accompanying booklet to coincide with a community program, "Gospel Quartet Heritage Day," held at Hamilton High School on July 31, 1983, in honor of Black gospel quartet singing in Memphis. The program and album both featured six of the groups with whom I had worked closely: the Spirit of Memphis, the Harps of Melody, the Pattersonaires, the Holy Ghost Spirituals, the Harmonizers, and the Gospel Writers.

In many ways this book is a continuation of the research that I began in the fall of 1979 in the Virginia Tidewater. While working on a project for the city of Newport News, I interviewed several gospel quartet singers and gathered information on such renowned local and regional groups as the Peerless Four Quartet and the

Silver Leaf Quartet of Norfolk. In a larger sense, this book is an extension and expansion of my research in Afro-American music, which began in 1968 with an interest in blues and has since come to encompass jazz and gospel in addition to other forms of black folk music.

My primary concern is in placing a specific musical style within its historical and cultural framework—an approach that could be called "the study of a musical culture." Unlike the majority of ethnomusicological studies published prior to the 1950s, which emphasize field recording and subsequent analysis of the music,[9] this book, like Gerhard Kubik's on a contemporary African group in Malawi, is more concerned with music as a cultural phenomenon.[10] Such a cultural approach has become more prevalent among ethnomusicologists over the past thirty years as they draw ideas from folklorists, anthropologists, and linguists. During this period ethnomusicologists have also come to a greater appreciation and understanding of the cultural and social aspects of their own research.

This study represents a multifaceted account of religious musical expression in a city noted for its blues, jazz, and soul music. Black music in Memphis is often equated with Frank Stokes, Booker T and the MGs, George Coleman, Sam and Dave, Will Shade, Phineas Newborn, or any number of other equally well respected black artists. Gospel quartet singers have created yet another vital form of Afro-American music in Memphis—one with its own unique musical heritage, spatial patterns, aesthetics, and history.

"Happy in the Service of the Lord" relates the story of a special musical community, its members, and their notable contributions to the cultural and musical identity of Memphis. Perhaps more than any other of the musical communities with which I have worked, black quartet singers in Memphis integrate their music into everyday life; indeed, many of them try to live the life about which they sing. Several of them have been singing and laboring within this unique community for over fifty years, for rewards that are almost entirely spiritual. This book and its companion High Water recordings pay them a small tribute, which they have earned many times over and so richly deserve.

NOTES

1. See, for example, Irene Jackson, *Afro-American Religious Music: A Bibliography and a Catalogue of Gospel Music* (Westport, Conn.: Greenwood Press, 1979), for a listing of work in this field.

2. Portia Maultsby, review of *Jubilee to Gospel: A Selection of Commercially Recorded Black Religious Music, 1921–1952,* JEMF-108, in *Ethnomusicology,* 27 (1983), p. 162.

3. For a listing of the work on this music, see Kip Lornell, "Afro-American Gospel Quartets: An Annotated Bibliography and LP Discography of Pre-War Recordings," *JEMF Quarterly,* 17 (1981), pp. 19–24.

4. Horace Boyer, "Gospel Music," *Music Educators Journal,* 42 (1978), p. 34.

5. Pearl Williams-Jones, "Afro-Gospel Music," in *Development of Materials for a One Year Course in African Music for the General Undergraduate Student,* ed. Veda Butcher (Washington, D.C.: Howard University, 1970), pp. 202–3.

6. David Evans, "The Roots of Afro-American Gospel Music," *Jazzforschung,* 8 (1976), pp. 124–25.

7. *The New Grove Dictionary of Music and Musicians,* vol. 12, ed. Stanley Sadie (London: Macmillan, 1980), p. 346.

8. For further information on the cultural importance and styles of black American gospel music, see Horace C. Boyer, "Contemporary Gospel," *The Black Perspective in Music,* 7 (no. 1, Spring 1979), pp. 5–59; Paul Oliver, "Black Gospel Music," in *The New Grove Dictionary of Music and Musicians,* vol. 10, ed. Stanley Sadie (London: Macmillan, 1980), pp. 254–59; and Wyatt Tee Walker, *"Somebody Calling My Name": Black Sacred Music and Social Change* (Valley Forge, Pa.: Judson Press, 1979), pp. 127–73.

9. Two examples by Francis Densmore are *Chippewa Music* (Washington, D.C.: Smithsonian Institution, 1910) and *Nootka and Quileute Music* (Washington, D.C.: Smithsonian Institution, 1939).

10. Gerhard Kubik, *The Kachamba Brothers Band: A Study of Neo-Traditional Music in Malawi* (Manchester, England: University of Manchester Press, 1974).

"One Hundred Years of Harmony Singing"

Black American gospel quartet singing is a distinctly twentieth-century musical and cultural phenomenon with clear roots in the traditional and popular music of the Reconstruction era. Since that time, the quartet tradition has traversed an interesting path from its southern folk roots to the heights of popular music during the 1940s and 1950s. This chapter provides an overview of the hundred-year odyssey of Afro-American religious quartets.

Despite all the research that has been done on black American music, it is difficult to specify the precise cultural, geographical, and musical origins of religious quartet singing. It is evident that college jubilee singing groups formed during the last third of the nineteenth century provided one of the earliest sources for quartets. More productively, however, our search should begin with the all-black minstrel shows that were formed at the beginning of Reconstruction.

Minstrel shows in themselves are a fascinating part of American culture. Beginning in the 1830s, they presented a distorted vision of Afro-American plantation life to many people across the nation through music, comedy, jokes, dramatic sketches, and speeches. The lampoon was further heightened by white minstrel entertainers who appeared on stage with blackened faces. By the late 1840s minstrel shows were very popular among white northern audiences who had virtually no direct contact with southern Afro-American culture. However, what began as an Anglo-American parody of black culture gradually took on new meaning as blacks joined previously all-white troupes. Just after the Civil War adventurous entrepreneurs formed all-black minstrel shows, which proved successful and continued to draw crowds through at least the 1890s.

By the early 1870s both black and white minstrel shows had been codified into a three-part format, which is still used by the few remaining minstrel productions. The first part features music and humorous exchanges between several comedians (endmen) and a straightman (interlocutor). Part two, a variety section known as the "olio," highlights such diverse talents as jugglers, acrobats, clowns, ventriloquists, and "stump" speakers, who pepper their speeches with malapropisms and mispronunciations. The final section consists of a one-act skit, often in a plantation setting. Minstrel shows proved to be one of the most popular entertainment forms until the turn of the century and are still put on by Lions clubs in Covington and Vinton, Virginia.[1]

The musical portion of the pre–Civil War minstrel shows included instrumental numbers performed on fiddles, jawbones, and banjos, as well as vocalists singing a wide range of traditional and popular material. Some of the vocals were rendered by "quartettes."[2] Although few individual blacks appeared in minstrel shows prior to the Civil War, the importance of blacks in minstrelsy after 1865 is well documented.[3] Reconstruction offered new opportunities for cultural, legal, and economic advancements for blacks, despite the bitter realities of the Ku Klux Klan, voter taxes, and many other social barriers.

Minstrel shows reached the height of popularity in the post–Civil War era, and no doubt there were scores of quartets that appeared with these troupes, large and small, though we really know very little about them. Ike Simond, a black entertainer who worked with minstrel shows during the 1870s and 1880s, listed a dozen delightfully named black quartets associated with popular entertainment: Sans Souci, Olympic, Climax, Twilight, Garden City, Excelsior, Mountain Pink, Beethoven, Eclipse, Buckeye, Black Diamond, and Dark Town Quartette.[4] The famous ragtime composer Scott Joplin briefly sang with a minstrel group in his home state of Missouri during the early 1890s, as did W. C. Handy, in his native Mississippi and later in Birmingham, Alabama.

While Reconstruction minstrel show quartets were touring the South, predominantly black schools were creating innovative singing ensembles known as "jubilee groups." In some instances, most notably Fisk University, the school and its jubilee singing groups were formed almost simultaneously. The majority of these institutions were located in the South and include many still-thriving institutions such as Atlanta University, Southern University (Baton Rouge, Louisiana), Livingstone College (Salisbury, North Carolina), and Hampton University (Hampton, Virginia).

One of the era's most demanding challenges was to educate the several million primarily illiterate blacks emancipated following the Civil War. The response was the creation of dramatically underfunded, segregated school systems that stressed basic skills like reading, writing, and arithmetic in addition to vocational courses like sewing and shoemaking. On a post secondary level, the American Missionary Association of New York founded seven institutions of higher education, one of the first of which was Fisk University in Nashville, Tennessee.

In 1871, within five years of its founding, Fisk sponsored a tour by its first troupe of "jubilee singers"—a term the university may have coined to celebrate the freedom blacks gained after emancipation—to help promote and raise money for the financially troubled school. George White, who served as teacher, treasurer, and choir director, traveled north with the Fisk Jubilee Singers, many of whom were former slaves. Their initial stop in Cincinnati was plagued by low attendance, inadequate financial returns, and mounting expenses. But thanks to favorable newspaper reviews, sympathetic clergy, and support from the northern black community, the tour gained momentum and ended as a financial and critical success. The tours continued during the 1870s, and by the spring of 1873 the Fisk Jubilee Singers were ready to embark on a trip to England, where they performed in London and many small cities. Their exotic style of singing and the novelty of seeing and hearing former slaves from America drew immense crowds. The tour proved wildly successful and was the first of many the Fisk Jubilee Singers would take.[5]

The financial and critical triumphs of the Fisk singing group did not escape the notice of other struggling, predominantly black schools. Many of these institutions looked to the Fisk Jubilee Singers, who raised hundreds of thousands of dollars, as a public relations model to emulate during the late nineteenth century. Hampton University was perhaps the first of Fisk's peers to take the jubilee singing movement seriously. In the late 1870s Hampton began sending out their own musical ambassadors.

The prosperity of the university jubilee singing groups inevitably stirred the spirit of American entrepreneurship. Within a year of forming the Fisk ensemble, George White expressed concern that the name "jubilee singers" was being exploited by other commercial groups hoping to cash in on the widespread interest in this music. The blossoming of the Fisk and other school groups, such as those sponsored by Straight University of New Orleans, Morehouse College of Atlanta, Georgia, Tuskegee Institute of Tuskegee, Alabama, and Utica Institute of Utica, Mississippi, possibly helped to reinforce the popularity of the minstrel quartets and jubilee groups that flourished between 1870 and 1910.

The true dimensions of the school jubilee singers movement are unclear, though these groups were certainly important for several decades. The *Chicago Defender,* which included many references to university and college jubilee groups well into the 1930s, noted in its August 12, 1911, issue that the "Claflin [Texas] University Jubilee Singers, who have been on the road for the past *nine years,* and who have been singing in and about the city [Chicago] for the past two weeks at the big churches, will give their farewell concert next Thursday evening at 9 o'clock, Aug. 17th" (emphasis added). On March 5, 1927, this same paper observed that the West Virginia Collegiate Glee Club had recently completed a fund-raising tour that was "attended by persons prominently connected in New York's most exclusive social, musical, and collegiate circles." Such references make the intent of these groups abundantly clear, particularly in their pursuit of the money concentrated in northern urban centers.

Although they followed in the footsteps of the larger jubilee ensembles, university quartets were by no means lesser stepchildren. Most of the schools with jubilee groups also sponsored quartets, as did many of the newer institutions, such as Livingstone College, that were founded after 1900. The earliest references to quartets are found in the Hampton University Archive. Among the archive's holdings are photographs of the Hampton Institute Quartet from the middle 1880s, cylinder recordings of several quartet performances dating from approximately 1898, and printed programs. The quartet apparently was an active force in the school's fund-raising efforts until it was disbanded in 1945.

Another early institutional group, the Dinwiddie Colored Quartet, was recorded by the Victor Company. The group was formed just before the turn of the century to sing on behalf of the John A. Dix Industrial School in Dinwiddie, Virginia. Typically, the quartet performed at school fund-raisers, though it appears that by 1902 it had moved to the vaudeville stage.[6] Like other quartets of the time, the Dinwiddie group was formed for at least two reasons, one of which was purely financial and pragmatic: if jubilee groups could raise money for their sponsoring institutions, then quartets could do the same at a much smaller cost. The development of college quartets also may have paralleled the general popularity of the touring minstrel show quartets. By the turn of the century both college and minstrel quartets were extremely potent musical forces in the black community.

While there is evidence to support the popularity of these quartets, what else do we know about them and their music? From the pioneering recordings of the Fisk Jubilee Quartet, the Dinwiddie Colored Quartet, and Polk Miller's Old South Quartette between 1902 and 1913, it is possible to make some general observations regarding performance styles. These groups stressed clear diction and precise pronunciation; and they offered little vocal embellishment or improvisation as well as only occasional instances of syncopation or rhythmic ornamentation. The vocal timbre of many of the singers was very reminiscent of more formally trained musicians, and most of their songs were homophonic in texture, often vacillating between major and minor tonalities.

Minstrel and institutional groups alike certainly performed a mixed, rather eclectic repertoire consisting of secular and sacred songs. The secular numbers included songs composed by Stephen Foster, like "Old Black Joe" and "My Old Kentucky Home," humorous ditties, traditional material, "coon" songs like "Old Jemima," "Way Down Yonder in the Cornfield," and "Little Alabama Coon," and patriotic songs. The religious songs were primarily spirituals like "Roll, Jordan, Roll" and "You May Talk about Jerusalem Morning," in addition to contemporary jubilee-style numbers.

It appears that there might be some stylistic parallels between contemporary white quartets and these college and minstrel black quartets, possibly due to the fact that the black groups were performing for a popular, racially mixed audience and thus downplayed the more traditional elements in their singing. In fact, the most distinctly Afro-American traits these recordings display is a "call and response" textual organization. But it would be misleading to suggest that Afro-American quartet singing was limited to the minstrel stage and college groups. There is always interaction among the various levels of culture, and the truth is that quartets were also part of black folk music during the late nineteenth century.

The earliest reference to this tradition in folk culture is also the first reference to black religious singing by a "quartette." While traveling through Virginia in June 1851, Frederika Bremer reported: "I heard the slaves, about a hundred in number, singing at their work in large rooms; they sang in quartettes . . . in such perfect harmony, and with such exquisite feeling, that it was difficult to believe them self-taught."[7] Another early account of what might be heterophony among slave singers, or at the very least a foreshadowing of four-part harmony, states:

> There is no singing in parts, as we understand it, and yet no two seem to be singing the same thing; the leading singer starts the words of each verse, often improvising, and others, who "base" him as it is called, strike in with the refrain or even join in the solo when the words are familiar. And the "basers" themselves seem to follow their own whims, beginning where they please, striking an octave above or below, or hitting some other note that chords, so as to produce the effect of a marvelous complication and variety and yet with the most perfect time and rarely with any discord.[8]

The noted black scholar James Weldon Johnson penned the first indisputable reference to folk quartet singing within the Afro-American community. In reminiscing about his Florida childhood during the 1890s, Johnson recalled:

> Pick up four colored boys or young men anywhere and the chances are ninety out of a hundred that you have a quartet. Let one of them sing the melody and others will naturally find the parts. Indeed, it may be said that all male Negro youth of the United States is divided

into quartets. When I was fifteen and my brother was thirteen we were singing in a quartet which competed with other quartets. In the days when such a thing as a white barber was unknown in the South, every barbershop had its quartet and the young men spent their leisure time "harmonizing."[9]

Finally, music historian Deac Martin recounts his experience of learning harmony singing from Missouri blacks just after the turn of the century:

In the darkness under the park's trees a voice would lead out a melody. The deep voice of Bud, a shoeshiner by vocation in the barber's shop, a voice recognized throughout the community, would chime in foundation harmony, and the other parts would slide in their grooves. Whether only four parts were at a sing out or a dozen were [singing], nobody other than Bud sang bass.

Many of the songs were held over from long-forgotten originals in which they pieced scraps of their own melody, harmony, and lyrics, as did the white barbershop quartets. Charlie Dimmit, a man of all work for the Dimmit Family, usually led . . . that is, he sang melody. . . . It is [not] possible to reduce their singing to notation [because] . . . notes cannot reproduce the effects of their rubato when a note is shortened in order to sustain another note. Nor is it possible to indicate the shadings when Bud, as example to others, would hold back to let the others dominate, then let go with a bass note . . . that almost twisted the nearby railroad track.[10]

These primary accounts strongly suggest that a tradition of quartet singing within the black community began prior to 1900. Barbershops, drugstores, and other points of commerce often provided an arena for harmony singing by the men and women of the community. Some of these groups were probably informal neighborhood quartets, while others no doubt practiced and performed their sentimental, sacred, and popular songs regularly. Indisputable evidence reveals that black quartet singing existed at every level of black culture by the turn of the century.[11]

Another genre of American music, shape-note singing, also influenced black quartets. Shape-note singing is a system of notated music commonly using four or seven shapes in lieu of the "round notes" found in standard European notation. Each shape is assigned a solfège syllable (i.e., fa, sol, la) to facilitate learning the system, which was first taught to blacks in southern "singing schools" during Reconstruction. Shape-note singing among blacks has been strongest in Mississippi, Alabama, and Georgia,[12] and its impact on black harmony quartets seems to be in its components rather than the general popularity of the tradition itself. Doris Dyen's study of black shape-note singing in Alabama suggests two components: the tendency of these singers to "improvise separate lines of harmonic accompaniment" and their "partly improvised, orally transmitted version of written harmony."[13] It is also note-worthy that both shape-note singing and black harmony quartets stress four-part harmony, utilize a training system, and have formal performance contexts.

White singers also performed in folk and popular quartets. Barbership quartets were the predominant form of Anglo-American harmony singing, with roots that can be traced to the 1880s.[14] These groups proved so popular following the turn of the century that clubs, fraternal organizations, churches, and companies like Westinghouse and 7-Up sponsored them. Tin Pan Alley and vaudeville were also strong contemporary forces in American popular music, and the barbershop quartets' sentimentality fit in perfectly. Several barbershop and other related popular quartets, including Edison, Peerless, and American, recorded commercial discs early in the century, but by the Great Depression the fad had largely passed.

The immense popular appeal of the jubilee groups, minstrel quartets, and barbership crooners charged the atmosphere for the widespread appreciation of small group religious harmony singing among blacks. After the turn of the century, community-based black gospel quartets sprang up throughout the South and over the next thirty years greatly increased in popularity as part of a working-class cultural movement. Religious quartet singing was incorporated into the everyday life of many blacks. These groups performed not only in churches but for special afternoon and evening programs, as Kerill Rubman notes:

> Factory and construction workers, porters, and other employees sang in company or union-affiliated quartets, performing at picnics, parties, dances, and other business or community events. Family members formed quartets. Negro colleges continued to sponsor such groups, and Baptist and Methodist churches often formed male quartets to sing sacred music at worship services and evening programs. In short, by the 1920s . . . harmonized *a cappella* quartet

singing was well established as a beloved and respected activity for musically adept black men [and women].[15]

These trends were directly tied with the increasingly urban character of the South's black population. During the first two decades of the twentieth century, for example, many blacks moved into metropolitan Norfolk, Virginia, from the surrounding rural areas of Virginia and North Carolina in a search for steady, lucrative blue-collar jobs in the shipyards and small factories. With this influx of potential talent it is not coincidental that Norfolk developed into one of the best-documented centers for quartet singing by the 1920s. Norfolk's significance is recalled by Thurmon Ruth of the Selah Jubilee Singers:

> . . . Norfolk, Virginia, that used to be a quartet town! I used to want to go to Norfolk because they told me that you could just be in bed at night and put your head out the window and guys would be on the corner blending, harmonizing. That's what the Norfolk Jubilee Singers told me. I believe the first quartet record I heard was Melvin Smith [the Silver Leaf Quartet of Norfolk] and he came out of Norfolk, [it was] "Sleep on, Mother." The Golden Gate originated in Norfolk and the Norfolk Jubilee Singers—they don't come any better.[16]

A similar situation was developing in Birmingham, Alabama, where the rapidly burgeoning coal and iron industry helped to attract 100,000 blacks between 1890 and 1920. Many of these newcomers settled in the dingy, diffuse company towns of Bessemer and Fairfield. As Doug Seroff observes: "Community life within the mining camps, company quarters, and other segregated black settlements around Bessemer [was] unusually rich in fellowship. Mass immigration brought together a variety of regional experience in the singing of traditional spirituals. Quartets were organized in the churches . . . and in the schools and places of work. Denied access to other forms of popular entertainment and diversion, quartet singing became a general pastime for Jefferson County's black youth."[17]

To some degree this pattern was repeated in cities across the South. While Birmingham and Norfolk stand out as the prime examples, other cities like Atlanta and Jacksonville also had strong early community quartet traditions. Following the "great migration" of southern blacks to urban centers in the North after World

War I, cities like Detroit, Chicago, and Cleveland gradually became strongholds for quartet singing.[18]

Significantly, schools at all levels played a strong role in encouraging black religious harmony singing, which was considered dignified and worthwhile by Afro-American schoolteachers, many of whom were educated at southern black colleges. Numerous quartet singers received their initial harmony singing instruction in primary and secondary schools, and several outstanding quartets evolved out of this milieu. The Golden Gate Quartet began singing together as students at the Booker T. Washington High School in Norfolk, Virginia, in the middle 1930s. The Five Blind Boys of Mississippi first met while attending the Piney Woods School during the late 1930s.

The experiences of R. C. Foster of Bessemer, who began training quartets in Jefferson County, Alabama, in 1915, well illustrate the links between schools and community-based quartets:

> I was in school under a young man graduated from Tuskegee who learned to sing there, and he taught me quartet music. Professor Vernon W. Barnett . . . was a black man and he come out to teach a little small school; that was the Charity High Industrial School in Lowndes County, Alabama. A certain portion of the day we had practice. We called it voice culture. You could hear the four voices but they was so even that if you were sitting out there you couldn't hardly tell who was singing what. And it come down just like one solid voice and it sounded just like a brass band![19]

Quartet singing was respectable because it was so closely combined with "positive" aspects of culture: education, family, place of employment, and, above all, the church. Certainly the involvement of blacks with quartets also made the transition from their rural birthplaces to the nation's urban centers easier. Blues singing was yet another musical form that helped to ease the social dysfunction felt by Afro-Americans moving to the city. This seemed to be especially true for younger males, many of whom turned to the "devil's music" for comfort and self-expression; other singers vacillated between the two worlds. But quartets provided an important, acceptable social and musical outlet.[20]

These grassroots quartets also offered singers a musical alternative to the institutional and minstrel show groups. Community quartets incorporated stylistic elements from these and other allied traditions to form a new genre. The gospel quartet style that emerged early in this century—indeed, gospel music itself—was a hybrid. Unlike their predecessors, gospel quartets stressed rhythmic inventiveness, a strong sense of syncopation, and the use of many vocal techniques, such as growls, slurs, and falsetto, incorporated from their folk background. These groups also used many newly composed songs along with the traditional material and spirituals. It must have been striking to hear a spiritual like "Rollin' through an Unfriendly Land" sung for the first time in the emerging gospel style.

The widespread and rapidly growing popularity of these quartets was not lost on America's mass media, particularly the record companies. Although Columbia recorded the Standard Quartette as early as 1895, and Victor followed with the Dinwiddie Colored Quartet in 1902, these cylinders and discs were poorly distributed. It was not until the early 1920s that record companies more thoroughly mined the wealth of black religious quartet music.

These quartet recordings were part of a larger trend that included the documentation of many forms of American and ethnic traditional music. In fact, the record companies issued all of the pre-1922 quartet and jubilee recordings as part of a general popular series. In 1922, however, companies such as OKeh, Columbia, Paramount, and Gennett began recording many more black folk musicians, selling the recordings as part of a special segregated "race" series. The Columbia 14000, OKeh 8000, and Paramount 12/13000 series featured musicians as diverse as Bessie Smith, the Norfolk Jubilee Singers, Louis Armstrong, Blind Joe Reynolds, Blythes Blue Boys, Barbecue Bob, Marshall Owens, Lonnie Johnson, and the Delta Big Four.[21]

Among the earliest and most prolific of the community quartets to record commercially was the Norfolk Jubilee Singers. The quartet's initial records were for OKeh in 1921, but by 1923 the group had switched to the Paramount label. One of its earliest Paramount recordings, "Father Prepare Me" / "My Lord's Gonna Move This Wicked Race" (Paramount 12035), was so popular that it remained in the catalog for nine years, until the company went out of business in 1932. Paramount's success almost certainly inspired other companies, as dozens of community quartets were recorded during southern field sessions that became common practice among record companies by the late 1920s. These sessions brought most of the major companies into southern cities such as Atlanta, Memphis, New Orleans, and San Antonio, where many types of local talent, including quartets, were documented.

An equally important outlet for the promotion and dissemination of black gospel quartet singing was the radio. Quartets began performing on "live" broadcasts at about the same time as they began recording in large numbers for the commercial record companies. Virtually all of the programs on these early radio stations were live, and the talent included hillbilly musicians, drama, dance bands, comedy, and gospel quartets. In Roanoke, Virginia, for example, the N & W Imperial Quartet was broadcasting over WDBJ as early as 1928, an activity mirrored in the tidewater region where local groups like the Silver Leaf Quartet of Norfolk and the Golden Crown Quartet began their radio work at about the same time.

Local businesses underwrote many of these daily or weekly fifteen- to thirty-minute radio shows, which brought the singing groups wider exposure. As the number and geographical distribution of quartets performing on local and regional stations prior to World War II grew, the broadcasts' impact also increased. During the 1930s several quartets began appearing on nationally syndicated programs. The Utica Jubilee Quartet was featured on one of the first such programs in 1927, over the National Broadcasting Network. It was soon followed by many other groups, including the Southernaires, whose show, "The Little Weather Beaten Church of the Air," ran from 1933 to 1944.

Grassroots gospel quartets had grabbed the musical imagination of black America by the time the Great Depression settled over the country. Although the record industry was decimated by the depression, Columbia and OKeh continued to distribute recordings by a few select groups. Meanwhile, the radio broadcasts of other quartets continued to reach hundreds of thousands of listeners, no doubt including a significant number of white Americans. Thus black gospel quartet singing began its rapid transformation from a religious, regional genre to a form of popular entertainment that was being heard across the United States.

The gospel quartet tradition soon established itself as a vibrant, exciting, and new style of religious music. Its far-flung appeal partially began when the older spirituals and hymns were synthesized and infused with extended, innovative harmonies (embellished far beyond the basic triad and seventh), vocal improvisations, which included much crossing of the inner voices, prominent bass sing- ing, and strong falsetto singing from the high tenor. Quartets were also quick to include many of the popular religious songs newly composed by Thomas A. Dorsey, Lucie E. Campbell, and W. Her- bert Brewster during the 1920s and 1930s.

This distinctive combination won many fans for black gospel quartet singing. The confluence of the quartets' widespread popu- larity with mass media's attention soon promoted this music be- yond its initial audience of southern blacks. By the mid- to late 1930s, some black gospel quartets were headed toward full-time professional status. While groups from Texas, such as the Soul Stir- rers, and Birmingham's Famous Blue Jay Singers and Kings of Har- mony were key quartets during this transition, it was Norfolk's Golden Gate Quartet that was the single most influential group to take this major step.

Most musicians credit the Golden Gate Quartet with reinfusing the jubilee style with new life by adding an infectious, very rhyth- mic aspect to gospel singing. Thurmon Ruth, for instance, recalls: "the first I know it came from . . . the Gates."[22] Willie Johnson, founder of the Golden Gate Quartet, described it as "vocal percus- sion": "Any music that had a beat and had a joyful sound to it. It was a joyous sort of thing. I mean it was a thing you patted your foot by. It wasn't a thing that made you want to cry, like 'my mama's dead and gone.' . . . It was all light really, entertaining. And it had some merit, like in the narrative tunes, a lot of people had never heard about all the Biblical heroes. They could hear the story start and they'd see when it reached the middle and they'd see it reach the apex and then quit."[23]

This modern jubilee style of gospel quartet singing contained both lyrical and musical innovations. The words of jubilee quartet performances often told a coherent story based on a parable from the Bible; for example, two of the Golden Gates' best-known songs describe the trials of Job and Noah. The fact that jubilee songs fea- tured a story-line appealed to listeners, possibly because it was something different in black music tradition. Unlike the blues, which is nonlinear and coheres through emotional logic, jubilee songs are closer to sermons that are presented in a more thematic or narrative form. The latter also include the "pumping" bass, interjected falsetto tenor singing, dramatic *cante fable* lead vocal, and the simple polyrhythms and well-placed syncopations that characterize modern jubilee quartet singing.

Expanding from its home base in Norfolk, Virginia, the Golden Gate Quartet began touring across the Southeast. By 1936 the group was on the road most of the time and was broadcasting regularly over WIS in Columbia, South Carolina. Within a year this radio work led the group into the studio of Bluebird Records, for whom it recorded for three years. Just before World War II the group landed a recording contract with Columbia, and in the early 1940s the Golden Gate Quartet broadcast regularly over the NBC radio network. It gradually expanded its repertoire in order to move into the lucrative pop music field and by the middle 1940s had toured with several white and black swing bands, appearing at the White House and performing at New York City's famous Café Society. In short, by the close of World War II the Golden Gate Quartet had become "the most artistically innovative, widely imitated, and the most commercially successful of all twentieth-century religious quartets."[24]

The role of gospel quartets like the Famous Blue Jay Singers and the Soul Stirrers during the late 1930s' transition period to full-time, professional status was critical to groups that followed in their footsteps. During the middle 1930s the Famous Blue Jay Singers and the Kings of Harmony moved their base of operations from Jefferson County, Alabama, to Dallas, Texas, where they eventually met Houston's Five Soul Stirrers. These three groups were among the first to give up the security of full-time employment in exchange for the potentially lucrative but untried life of professional gospel quartet singing. While the Kings of Harmony chose to remain in the South, the Famous Blue Jay Singers and the Soul Stirrers wanted a more central home from which to tour. By 1940 they had settled in Chicago, which allowed them greater access to the important northern urban market.

Like the Golden Gate Quartet, these groups were also innovators. They pioneered the use of "switch leading," which called for more than one lead singer during a song. Role switching in mid-performance often ignited the lead singers, helping to create a competitive atmosphere, and frequently led to even more emotional performances. Dual lead singing also expanded many quartets from four to five members. The popularity of these groups soon led to the practice of billing shows as "song battles" in order to build up an even larger crowd. These new performance techniques, creative marketing tactics (such as multiple "star" billing on a single program), and successful records and radio programs by the Golden Gate Quartet, Mitchell's Christian Singers, and others laid a very strong foundation for the mass popularity of quartets.

The onset of World War II slowed the rapidly growing interest in quartets. Gasoline rationing and a shortage of rubber for tires greatly inhibited travel, while the record industry was virtually shut down for nearly a year and a half by a shellac shortage and a bitter dispute between the musicians' union and the record companies. The only aspect of quartet singing not affected by the war was radio broadcasting; in fact, groups sought out even more radio exposure due to the travel and recording restrictions. One quartet that particularly benefited from the continued boom in broadcasting was Nashville's Fairfield Four: "They began broadcasting over 50,000 watt WLAC in 1942, after winning a local contest sponsored by Colonial Coffee. In later years they were sponsored by Sunway Vitamins. Their WLAC program was transcribed and broadcast over powerful sister stations from Philadelphia to Salt Lake City, Utah, effectively blanketing the nation. Their broadcasts were so popular that the group was in constant demand for personal appearances and soon became the South's greatest box office attraction."[25]

It is important to understand that the radio broadcasts themselves were not very lucrative, but the live engagements that resulted from such exposure did provide a substantial income for the group. And the Fairfield Four was not an isolated example of radio's power. The Four Harmony Kings, formed in West Virginia in 1938, built their reputation through radio work and personal appearances. Within three months the group moved from a weekly Sunday morning show to a fifteen-minute daily radio program on WNOX in Knoxville, which covered much of the southeastern United States. After the Swan Bread Company began sponsoring the radio show, the group changed its name to the Swan Silvertone

Singers.[26] At the same time the Selah Jubilee Singers built a career by way of daily radio work over WPTF, a clear channel 50,000-watt station in Raleigh, North Carolina.

Beginning in mid-1944 the record industry reopened. Unlike the early days, which were dominated by half a dozen companies, hundreds of independent record labels appeared during the mid- to late 1940s. The shellac shortages and the musicians' union's recording ban had shaken the industry to the core and opened it up to entrepreneurs who recorded almost every type of music in America. While a very few companies like Peacock (Houston) and King (Cincinnati) became major labels, most remained one-person operations that released a handful of records before going out of business.

Despite such things as lack of promotion, questionable accounting practices, and inferior pressings, many groups sought the opportunity to record their music, while others assiduously avoided the recording studios, apparently fearful that they would be defrauded or that some other group might steal an arrangement from one of their records. In most ways, though, the radio and record industries served the interests of quartets by getting their names and music before a wide audience. Both of these media helped to expand the groups' audience, but live concerts, programs, and personal appearances provided the quartets with real financial stability.

What did all of this media attention actually mean to quartet singing? Prior to World War II only a select few of the thousands of black gospel quartets performed professionally. After the war ended and the popularity of quartets skyrocketed, the cultural and musical climate grew ripe for full-time performing. Interest in this type of music became so great that by the late 1940s there were "hundreds of quartets making lengthy tours, travelling around the country singing in churches, school auditoriums, and concert halls."[27] The organizational, social, and cultural fiber of quartet singing thus underwent a critical transformation as the result of this newfound mass appeal. The network of community quartets still existed, of course, but many singers joined or formed groups, while other quartets decided to test their popularity on the road. Quartets during this era had to provide a strong and varied repertoire of "deep harmony" numbers featuring complex, ever-shifting harmonies and powerful gospel tunes in order to sustain interest during a live program. There were so many fine jubilee-style harmony groups around that only the very best caught the audiences' attention for very long.[28]

The jubilee groups spawned many imitators on the East Coast. The Golden Gate Quartet in particular became *the* model for innumerable quartets in the Carolinas, Virginia, Maryland, and the urban corridor between Washington, D.C., and New York City. Many groups also copied Willie Johnson's Bible narratives and syncopated bass arrangements. By the late 1940s a new style, "hard gospel," began to catch on ("hard" referring to the emotional, powerful lead singing epitomized by Ira Tucker of the Dixie Hummingbirds and the Sensational Nightingales' Julius Cheeks). Highlighting lead vocals represented an innovation in quartet singing and acknowledged the influence of solo gospel singers like Mahalia Jackson, Rosetta Tharpe, and Alex Bradford.

Hard gospel quartets often highlighted songs by contemporary black religious songwriters like Lucie E. Campbell, Kenneth Morris, W. Herbert Brewster, and Thomas A. Dorsey. They frequently performed emotionally evocative arrangements that "worked" the crowd in an attempt to drive them to higher states of religious fervor. Such groups could also perform harmony numbers, but they made their biggest impact through sheer vocal power and mastery of their stage image. The gradual introduction of instruments (first guitars and pianos, then bass and drums), which important groups like the Swan Silvertone Singers and the Dixie Hummingbirds had incorporated by 1950, further heightened the visceral impact of their music.

By the early 1950s jubilee and hard gospel elements both proved so important that many groups included two separate lead singers—one for jubilee, the other for hard gospel. Sometimes groups with contrasting styles, for example, the Jubilaires and the Pilgrim Travelers, would appear on the same program, in a "song battle." This combination brought out even greater crowds, cheering for their favorite group and style. Such shows underscored the already intense competition found among the many fine grassroots, semiprofessional, and professional quartets singing after World War II.

The predominant trend of dressing in sharply tailored clothes, presenting a highly polished stage act using well-rehearsed choreography, and the addition of electronic instruments illustrates the quartets' desires to uphold a "professional" appearance. Their financial well-being and personal integrity were being judged every time they performed at a church or auditorium, and if they did not please the audiences, their careers were in jeopardy. Such pressures led to a gradual, perhaps inevitable, institutionalization or standardization in dress, stage presence, and performance style paralleling those of other professional entertainers. The importance of such changes were not lost on Thurmon Ruth:

> . . . I remember the time when groups dressed in black suits and white shirts and bow ties. Then we got to the place with red suits, green suits, loud as could get. Once upon a time I said I wouldn't wear certain colors and we ended up with some kelly green pants and some beige coats we had made in Chicago. Everybody said it was so sharp, you know . . . it impressed the ladies.
>
> We were entertainers, let's put it that way. We didn't try to get the folks to shout all that much; we entertained the folks—had a lot of novelty stuff. . . . They would call us "spirit killers," [because] we would do "Gospel Train," we'd shovel the coal; "There's Fire Down Below," we'd push him in the oven, throw him in the fire. It was hard for a group to beat us . . . [when] we could come along with our novelty stuff and cool 'em down.[29]

The Five Blind Boys of Mississippi and the Pilgrim Jubilees were in many respects the contemporary religious equivalent of Duke Ellington's famous Cotton Club Jungle Band or Whoopie John Wilfhart's Polka Band. Each group enjoyed professional status, a commercial recording contract, radio work, and a faithful and proud racial, ethnic, or regional audience. In the early 1950s black gospel quartets had such a strong base of popular support across the country that it seemed as if the musical genre would last forever.

The decade ending in 1955 marked the pinnacle of commercial success for Afro-American gospel quartets. Touring and personal appearances provided the primary financial support for major groups like the Dixie Hummingbirds, the Fairfield Four, the Harmonizing Four of Richmond (Virginia), and the Sensational Nightingales, which worked the urban centers as well as the small towns in the South. Other figures in black gospel music, like the Ward Singers, Roberta Martin, Brother Joe May, and Alex Bradford, enjoyed strong financial and popular support, too. There was a spirit of commercialism and showmanship pervading all of black gos-

Table 1. *The Emergence of Professional Quartets, 1935–60*

1935–40

Golden Gate Quartet	Norfolk, Virginia
Soul Stirrers	Houston, Texas
Kings of Harmony	Birmingham, Alabama
Famous Blue Jay Singers	Birmingham, Alabama

1940–50

Dixie Hummingbirds	Spartanburg, South Carolina
Spirit of Memphis	Memphis, Tennessee
Swan Silvertone	Charleston, West Virginia
Five Blind Boys of Mississippi	Jackson, Mississippi
Harmonizing Four	Richmond, Virginia
Fairfield Four	Nashville, Tennessee

1950–60

Flying Clouds of Joy	Detroit, Michigan
Bells of Joy	Houston, Texas
Sensational Nightingales	Greenville, South Carolina
Highway QCs	Houston, Texas

pel music as everyone tried to get their share of the money and the glory.

By the early 1950s professional quartets could be found throughout the South and in many northern cities. Table 1 lists the names and geographical origins of fourteen of the most important touring groups. The lure of full-time quartet singing was strong, even though touring meant leaving the secure confines of home for new places, new ideas, and temptations never before encountered. Life on the road was sometimes unpredictable and always changing, and financial security was never far from the singers' thoughts, for many of them were trying to support families. Doug Seroff observes, "When a group goes out on the road as a full-time occupation, money and its proper division among members can become a serious point of contention. Money was the cause of many bitter breakups during the 'Golden Age.'"[30]

Finances became an even greater factor as the business end of quartet singing grew more lucrative. Programs headlined by major groups usually included three or four acts and brought in thousands of dollars in a single night. Multistar events, or "caravans," took place in major venues like the Apollo Theater in New York City or Birmingham's Civic Center. These were well advertised and heavily promoted over local radio stations, in newspapers, and on posters and placards placed throughout the Afro-American community. Members of the local participating groups personally sold tickets and made them available through record and grocery stores, in barbershops, and at the door. They also encouraged fans to buy group pictures and phonograph records. This was big business, indeed, and provided an incentive for group members to carefully scrutinize all financial transactions.

Most programs followed a prescribed format and lasted five or six hours, sometimes longer if some of the quartets were particularly successful in working the crowd. Audience members showed great respect for their favorite performers and responded to the music by clapping their hands, stomping their feet, and dancing in the aisles. Although the program might be an occasion for religious worship and expression, it was also an event celebrating popular music. The crowds' reactions were very much akin to those that fans of the era's other popular music singers expressed. Surely this was not what the Soul Stirrers or the Famous Blue Jay Singers expected when they began touring twenty years earlier.[31]

Even with gospel quartets enjoying stunning popularity, many singers were not interested in following the glitter of professional singing. They preferred the security of their own community, jobs they already knew, and a familiar social milieu. The groups they formed were content with local fame, weekly radio broadcasts, and a ready-made audience. Many of these quartets no doubt had the talent but not the inclination for full-time singing careers. Grassroots quartets continued to prosper in their own communities, and the general success of quartets singing helped to reinforce their popularity.

By the middle 1950s commercial interest in black American gospel quartets quickly subsided, in part due to changes in musical tastes but also because of the inevitable saturation of the marketplace. By this time several of the lead singers featured with quartets had taken on a more prominent position in the fans' eyes—singers like Claude Jeter of the Swan Silvertone Singers, Cassietta George of the Brewster Singers, and Ira Tucker of the Dixie Hummingbirds, who became stars in their own right. The change in emphasis from quartets to a harmony ensemble with a featured lead singer signaled a shift in popular interest back to solo performers. There also began a trend toward larger ensembles, especially choirs and choruses. This movement took ten years to blossom, but by the late 1960s the Edwin Hawkins Singers, James Cleveland's groups, and other similar ensembles ruled the world of black popular religious music.

Equally significant, many of these lead singers left the gospel field completely to try their hands at popular music. The Soul Stirrers' Sam Cooke, for example, gradually moved from simply being a member of the group to "headliner" status and finally into the world of secular music, where he enjoyed a strong career until his death in 1964. Many other black pop singers began their careers performing with quartets, including Lou Rawls (Pilgrim Travelers), Brook Benton (Bill Langford Quartet), Joe Hinton (Spirit of Memphis), "Little" Johnny Taylor (Highway QCs), and O. V. Wright (Spirit of Memphis).

Entire quartets also left gospel music for the greater financial rewards of popular music. In the early 1940s one of the Hampton Institute quartets dropped out of religious music and became the Deep River Boys. Another long-standing quartet, the Selah Jubilee Singers, switched to rhythm and blues about 1953, recording as the Larks for Apollo Records. Similarly, the New Orleans Humming Four, one of the Crescent City's outstanding gospel quartets for many years, became The Hawks, recording for Imperial Records in the 1950s.[32] This switch from gospel quartet to pop group often came at the insistence of record company executives, who made convincing pitches for the monetary rewards. Don Robey (Peacock/Duke Records), Bernie Bessman (Apollo Records), and Lew Chudd (Imperial Records) were legendary in their efforts to convince gospel quartets to convert to secular music. Such conversions were not new, however, for as early as the 1890s college jubilee groups from Fisk University were at least partially abandoning sacred music in order to try to reach a greater audience both in this country and abroad. The large financial stakes and recording opportunities of the 1940s and 1950s only provided a greater incentive to switch.

Although the seductive lure of popular music by no means destroyed the black gospel quartet field, by the 1950s it was becoming increasingly difficult to differentiate between black secular and sacred harmony groups. Both religious and popular quartets were using more amplified instruments, and their performance styles had evolved into carefully choreographed, well-paced rituals designed to squeeze as much emotional response from the crowd as possible. This fascination and flirtation with popular trends may have increased the revenues of some groups, but it also helped bring about the popular decline of black gospel quartet music. The opportunities for live performances dropped off dramatically after 1955 and a significant number of quartets stopped touring. Many full-time groups dropped from these ranks to those of the semiprofessionals; other returned to community quartet status, finding employment outside of the music field. It had been a rewarding ten-year period for some quartet singers, perhaps too good in the eyes of some black churchgoers.[33]

The long-burning, bright light that had focused on quartet singers inevitably opened them up to criticism from some of the more conservative black church members. These spiritual folks slowly became dissatisfied with the increasing secularization of gospel music by quartets. They saw gospel quartets being treated like popular music stars, riding in large, expensive automobiles, wearing fine clothes, and making generous salaries. Many church members felt that some quartets had moved too far from the spirit and ideals of the Lord's teachings, causing them to look with disfavor upon the more commercial, ostentatious groups.[34]

Although very few quartets, most notably the Dixie Hummingbirds and the Soul Stirrers, remained on the road after 1960, harmony groups continue to be an important part of black religious music in America. Many older, once full-time professional groups, such as the Harmonizing Four of Richmond (Virginia) and the Spirit of Memphis, retreated to semiprofessional status and remain popular regional groups. Several other grassroots quartets have been active for at least fifty years. None of them ever reached the semiprofessional ranks, but the Royal Harmony Four (Memphis, Tennessee), the Sterling Jubilees (Bessemer, Alabama), and the Alabama and Georgia Quartet (Chicago, Illinois) have been singing since the early 1930s. The careers of these and other quartets are largely undocumented because few of them were ever known outside their communities.

With quartet singing all but out of the free-wheeling commercial market, the future of this type of music seems to lie with community quartets. Despite a timorous revival of interest in quartet singing since 1980, there are no sure signs that this music will ever again enjoy a strong base of commercial support. Small group harmony singing has been such a basic, important form of black religious music, though, that its impact will no doubt be felt for many years. This book underscores the irony that, at least in Memphis, black gospel quartet singing has moved full circle from the folk tradition to popular culture and back again. Perhaps this cycle will begin once more.

NOTES

1. Robert Toll, *Blacking Up: The Minstrel Show in Nineteenth-Century America* (New York: Oxford University Press, 1974), provides the best minstrel show history.

2. This reference infers the presence of four-voice vocal groups in minstrel shows as early as the 1850s. See Carl Wittke, *Tambo and Bones* (Durham, N.C.: Duke University Press, 1930), p. 177.

3. See, for example, Toll, *Blacking Up,* chap. 5.

4. Ike Simond, *Old Slack's Reminiscences and Pocket History of the Colored Profession from 1865–1891* (Chicago: by the author, 1891), p. 26.

5. A nineteenth-century history of this movement is J. B. T. Marsh, *The Story of the Jubilee Singers* (Cleveland: Cleveland Printing and Publishing Company, n.d.). Doug Seroff is currently preparing a definitive study of the Fisk Jubilee Singers, based on heretofore unexplored primary sources.

6. *Louisiana Weekly,* March 2, 1929, n.p.

7. Frederika Bremer, *The Homes of the New World: Impressions of America* (New York: Harper and Brothers, 1853), as quoted in Dena Epstein, *Sinful Tunes and Spirituals* (Urbana: University of Illinois Press, 1977), p. 164.

8. William Allen, Charles Ware, and Lucy Garrison, *Slave Songs of the United States* (1867; rpt., New York: Oak Publications, 1965), p. v.

9. James Weldon Johnson, "The Origins of the 'Barber Chord,'" *The Mentor,* February 1929, p. 53.

10. Deac Martin, *Book of Musical America* (New York: Prentice-Hall, 1970), pp. 243–44.

11. A similar assertion is made by David Evans, brochure notes, *Let's Get Loose,* New World 290 (New York, 1981), p. 2.

12. The most comprehensive work on black American shape-note singing is Doris Dyen, "The Role of Shape-Note Singing in the Musical Culture of Black Communities in Southeastern Alabama" (Ph.D. dissertation, University of Illinois, 1977). See also John Work, "Plantation Meistersinger," *Musical Quarterly,* 39 (1941), pp. 40–49; Walter Byrd, "The Shape-Note Singing Convention as a Musical Institution in Alabama" (Master's thesis, University of Alabama, 1962); and Joe Dan Boyd, "Judge Jackson: Black Giant of White Spirituals," *Mississippi Folklore Register,* 4 (1970), pp. 7–11.

13. Dyen, "Role of Shape-Note Singing," p. 5.

14. Personal correspondence, Val Hicks to Kip Lornell, December 12, 1982; and Deac Martin, "The Evolution of Barbershop Harmony," *Music Journal Annual,* 23 (1965), pp. 24, 106.

15. Kerill Rubman, "From 'Jubilee' to 'Gospel' in Black Male Quartet Singing" (Master's thesis, University of North Carolina, 1980), p. 35.

16. Thurmon Ruth, interviewed by Kip Lornell, Birmingham, Alabama, October 11, 1980.

17. Doug Seroff, "On the Battlefield," in *Repercussions,* ed. Geoffrey Haydon and Dennis Marks (London: Century Publishing, 1985), pp. 35–36.

18. Further information about these trends can be found in George Davis and Fred Donaldson, *Blacks in the United States: A Geographic Perspective* (Boston: Houghton Mifflin, 1975).

19. Seroff, "On the Battlefield," p. 37.

20. This issue is more fully discussed in Kip Lornell, "Black Folk Music in Piedmont North Carolina," in *North Carolina Folklore Reader,* ed. Daniel Patterson and Terry Zug (unpublished manuscript).

21. For more information on this aspect of the American record industry, see John Godrich and Robert Dixon, *Recording the Blues* (London: Studio Vista, 1970); and Ronald Foreman, "Jazz and Race Records, 1920–1932" (Ph.D. dissertation, University of Illinois, 1968).

22. Thurmon Ruth interview.

23. Doug Seroff, "The Continuity of the Black Gospel Quartet Tradition—In Harmony with the Black Community," paper read at the Baptist Sunday School Convention, Nashville, Tennessee, October 1982, p. 14.

24. Ibid., p. 13.

25. Ibid., p. 17.

26. Rubman, "From 'Jubilee' to 'Gospel,'" p. 88.

27. Seroff, "Continuity of the Black Gospel Quartet Tradition," p. 17.

28. For further information on this movement, consult album liner notes by Ray Funk, *Detroit Gospel,* Heritage 311 (Sussex, England, 1986) and *Atlanta Gospel,* Heritage 312 (Sussex, England, 1987); Lynn Abbott, *New Orleans Gospel Quartets,* Heritage 306 (Sussex, England, 1985); and Vaughan Webb, *The Hampton Roads Quartets Tradition,* BRI 009 (Ferrum, Virginia, 1988).

29. Thurmon Ruth interview.

30. Seroff, "Continuity of the Black Gospel Quartet Tradition," p. 18.

31. A fuller description of these attitudes can be found in Tony Heilbut, *The Gospel Sound: Good News and Bad Times* (New York: Simon and Schuster, 1985), chaps. 2, 3.

32. See Lynn Abbott, "The New Orleans Humming Four," *Whiskey, Women, and . . . ,* 13 (1983), pp. 4–8.

33. Viv Broughton, *Black Gospel: An Illustrated History of the Gospel Sound* (Dorset, England: Blandford Press, 1985), pp. 61–91, contains a detailed account of black gospel music between 1945 and 1960.

34. Ibid., pp. 91–106.

2

"We Are the Spirit of Memphis"

By the 1930s Afro-American gospel quartets were popular across the South and in northern urban centers. Radio stations were broadcasting live quartet performances and all of the major commercial record companies listed quartets among their roster of artists. Recent research has shown that the most influential early groups came from two of the strongholds for community-based quartets: Jefferson County, Alabama, and the Virginia Tidewater. But what of quartets in other parts of the South and in northern cities? Among southern cities Memphis, Tennessee, has proven to be one of the most tenacious and influential hearths for blues, rhythm and blues, and soul music. Gospel quartets also have been an integral, albeit largely overlooked, segment of Afro-American music in Memphis.

Predepression quartet singers in Memphis performed without instrumental accompaniment. The I.C. Glee Club, for instance, featured only a cappella numbers, and there are no accounts of any groups using instruments until the late 1930s. Although the I.C. group was the only local quartet to record during this era, it was one among many active music groups during the 1920s. Older singers also recall the Harmony Four, the Old Red Rose Quartet, the L. and N. (Louisville and Nashville Railroad) Quartet, the Hollywood Specials, and the Mount Olive Wonders. (The heritage of one other quartet, the Spirit of Memphis, also extends back to the 1920s and will be covered later in this chapter.) While there must have been many other quartets active prior to the Great Depression, their histories have been lost to the vicissitudes of time.

The black musical culture of the 1920s is not a complete enigma, however, for we do know something more substantial about the I.C. Glee Club, which the Illinois Central Railroad sponsored. At the time of their recordings for OKeh, the quartet was composed of C. H. Evans, a porter, as first tenor; R. S. Saunders, a laborer, as second tenor; E. L. Rhodes, a springman, as baritone; and L. S. Brown, a pipefitter's helper, as bass. Organized in 1927, the club existed until some time in the late 1930s. According to a spokesman for the railroad, the quartet sang for "churches, lodges and . . . for ICRR employee events at the Memphis shop."[1] That its members named their ensemble for a local company is not unique. Testimony that such a practice benefited both parties is evident in two other Memphis groups—the Orval Brothers (Construction Company) Quartet and the S. and W. (Construction Company) Quartet. Elsewhere one finds the TCI (Tennessee, Coal, Iron Company) Quartet of Birmingham, Chicago's Stevedores Quartet, and the N. and W. (Norfolk and Western Railroad) Imperial Quartet in Roanoke, Virginia.

Although other companies had musical associations, it is especially interesting to note that the Illinois Central Railroad in Memphis sponsored at least three other groups, including the I.C. Hummingbirds, the I.C. Harmony Boys, and the I.C. Quartet (Number Two). The most specific information on this complex of ensembles comes from Haywood Gaines, a retired Illinois Central employee who sang with the I.C. Quartet (Number Two) between 1928 and 1939. He suggests that the railroad felt quartets helped improve its corporate image by association with such upstanding Christian music organizations. Gaines further notes that while the Illinois Central's support for the groups was usually literally in name only, the company's rewards were far more substantial:

> The purpose of the company to have quartets was bringing back business to the I.C. passenger [trains]. Business had left, and that was bringing them back. Folks thought little of the railroad at that time —the passenger service. . . . To get them to come and ride with us, we had booster clubs and singers. The booster club was . . . an organization that gave different parties or entertainment. They would entertain and invite the general public. When we got them there,

we would impress upon them the necessity to use the railroad as transportation. We gave dances . . . had 500 or 600 people! That brought business back to the railroad.[2]

Another responsibility of the I.C. quartets was singing on the trains themselves. Gaines recalls that "the singing groups was active riding up and down the road. Folks would come in to hear them, and some would ride the train with them. They'd go from Chicago to New Orleans. Wherever they'd go, they'd have to have extra cars."[3] Not all of the quartets actually traveled "up and down the road" on such prestigious missions, however. The railroad company called upon only the I.C. Hummingbirds for this task, while other groups entertained people at booster club meetings in and around Memphis. Although the Missouri-Pacific Railroad, which also served Memphis, echoed this pattern of corporate boosterism, we know virtually no details of its workings.[4]

Not all of the early Memphis quartets affiliated with businesses. Most were allied with community churches or specific neighborhoods and stayed out of the more commercial network that was beginning to develop. The only direct impact from outside the city was personal contact with nearby rural quartets that occasionally traveled to Memphis for weekend performances. Such travel became more prevalent during the 1940s and 1950s when quartet singing reached its popular peak. That local black quartets frequently affiliated with specific churches was not surprising given the central role of the church in Afro-American social, economic, and religious life. For example, the Mount Olive Wonders, the first quartet with which Theo Wade sang in the late 1920s, consisted of church members who provided a cappella harmony singing for their congregation, for programs at other churches, and at "box-lunch" social events held at church members' homes.[5]

For those predepression quartets not directly connected with a church, there was nearly always some neighborhood or community affiliation. The Harmony Four are recalled as one of the most respected singing groups in south Memphis at the time. Led by Gus Miller, the quartet performed for neighborhood community groups and in churches throughout the city. The Old Red Rose Quartet from north Memphis also frequently sang in local homes during the evening. Another quartet from north Memphis, the Royal Harmony Four, was founded by Jack Miller and James Spriggens in about 1930 and remains active under Miller's leadership with primary support from a network of local inner-city churches.

The members of these and other similar groups worked in full-time extramusical jobs. Harmony quartet singing was one example of religious feelings that could be expressed during weekly rehearsals and at Sunday programs. The era of part-time singing and quartet activity that centered upon the church, neighborhoods, or businesses lasted well into the 1940s. For quartets like the Royal Harmony Four, Memphis's Afro-American gospel community has been their lifeblood for over fifty years.

The Spirit of Memphis in many ways encapsulates the history of gospel quartet activity in Memphis. The group, which included "Quartette" in its name for many years before dropping it in the late 1940s, is unquestionably the best known and most commercially successful home-grown black gospel group. Although the Spirit of Memphis celebrated its fiftieth anniversary in 1980, the passage of so many years has obscured the precise date of its origination. In the memory of the sole surviving founding member, James Darling, the quartet was established in the gloom of the early depression and consisted of Darling, Burt Perkins, Arthur White, and Arthur Wright.[6] The roots of the Spirit of Memphis are in the T. M. and S. Quartet, a name derived from the initials of the *T*ree of Life, *M*ount Olive, and *S*t. Matthew's Baptist churches, which the various group members attended (Darling himself belonged to the Tree of Life Baptist Church). If this quartet was indeed the first incarnation of the Spirit of Memphis, then the group can more accurately be dated to 1927 or 1928.

Such genealogical problems result from the ever-changing personnel of quartets, the lack of written records, and hazy memories. The founding date of a group is an important event for Afro-American gospel quartets, however, because lavish celebrations are held to honor and commemorate the anniversaries. Prestige is also attached to the number of years a group has remained together, which further heightens the group's importance.

Irrespective of the precise details, it appears that the Spirit of Memphis altered its name around 1930 in memory of Charles Lindbergh's 1927 flight across the Atlantic in the *Spirit of St. Louis.* James Darling relates the story:

When the group was named . . . it was named after the initials of the churches; and when we decided to organize into a quartet, we had to bring in some names. The night we had to bring in some names, I hadn't thought up a name until we got almost to [the house at] Looney and Second Street. That's where we were meeting, at Burt Perkins's house. I had a pocket handkerchief, had the Spirit of St. Louis in the corner. That's where the name really originated. I put down the Spirit of Memphis from this Spirit of St. Louis pocket hand-kerchief, you know, the design in the corner.[7]

This transformation in name, which symbolized a very con-scious move from a church-allied group to a quartet representing the city in which the members lived, foreshadowed some of the changes that were to take place in Memphis quartet singing. It was a presentiment that quietly signaled the gradual rise of profes-sionalism, which was the single most important alteration in the tradition. By publicly aligning itself with a well-known "worldly" event, this former church ensemble set the foundation for the slow evolution from grassroots to popular entertainment. It took nearly twenty years for Memphis groups to complete this process.

At the time the Spirit of Memphis adopted its present moniker, quartet singing was becoming more popular in the city. Although no Memphis groups are known to have recorded during the 1930s, the sheer number of groups indicate that quartet singing was wide-spread. Quartets active between 1930 and 1940 included the Orange Mound Harmonizers, the North Memphis Harmonizers, the Lake Grove Specials, the Gospel Writers, the Four Stars of Har-mony, the Middle Baptist Quartet, the Busyline Soft Singers, the True Friends Gospel Singers, the Veteran Jubilees, and the Indepen-dent Quartet. (A complete list of quartets is found in Appendix I.)

One of the more formidable groups from this era was the Middle Baptist Quartet, organized in 1935 and held in awe by most quar-tet veterans around Memphis. It was certainly one of the most re-vered of the unrecorded local quartets. In the late 1930s the quar-tet included James Darling, Mose Hill, Elijah Jones, and James Harvey, each reputedly a first-rate singer; in fact many people still recall with wonder Harvey's lead singing. The group, which also at various times included Gus Miller (the dean of the local trainers), James Strong, Sam Miller, and Horace Fisher, served as a train-ing ground for singers who left to join other respected harmony ensembles. It also was the foundation for yet another legendary quartet, the Gospel Writers.

The Gospel Writers played a critical role in Memphis gospel quartet history. The respect accorded them by their fellow singers testifies to their importance. But it was the leadership of their founder, Elijah Jones, who trained many harmony singers during his fifty-year career, that made the Gospel Writers a group of renown just prior to World War II. As a quartet trainer Jones helped to shape a distinctive local tradition through his suggestions regarding repertoire, vocal techniques, harmony, and arrangements.

The archetypal "sound" of Memphis quartets from the pre–World War II period is difficult to establish since the only recordings available from this period are the I. C. Glee Club's fourteen sides. It is possible to augment these vintage performances with songs recorded by four contemporary groups—the Harps of Melody, the Harmonizers, the Royal Harmony Four, and the Gospel Writers—who still consciously keep the older, a cappella style alive. (All but the Royal Harmony Four can be heard on discs released by High Water Records.)

The repertoires of these early unaccompanied quartets tend to rely heavily upon traditional material. For example, if the recordings by the I. C. Glee Club truly reflect their performing repertoire, then they mixed older spirituals with original songs based on traditional themes. The former category includes well-known pieces such as "I Shall Not Be Moved," "So Glad Trouble Don't Last Always," and "Lord Have Mercy When I Die"; into the latter category fall "If I Could Hear My Mother Pray Again" and "When They Ring Dem Golden Bells." Several other songs—"I'm Going Home on the Chickasaw Train," "Riding on the Seminole," and "Panama to Chi"—underscore the group's affiliation with the Illinois Central Railroad. It is also interesting to note that the motifs utilized in these songs, trains and travel, are two of the most popular images in black religious and secular folk music.[8]

Similar comments apply to the repertoires of the Harps of Melody, the Harmonizers, and the Gospel Writers of the 1980s. The principal difference in their singing is the inclusion of many more composed gospel songs like "I Need Thee," "I'm Leaning on the Everlasting Arms," or "Peace in the Valley." Nonetheless, most of their repertoires still consists of the traditional songs or spirituals.

The Harmonizers, for example, regularly perform "Steal Away" and use "Rollin' through an Unfriendly Land" as their theme song and introductory number. Elijah Ruffin, the Harmonizers' founder and trainer, knew that these songs were old, but he was surprised to learn that they were first "collected" during Reconstruction.[9]

The Gospel Writers still sing many of the arrangements that Elijah Jones taught them when he worked with the group during the late 1970s. According to George Rooks, who heard the "old" Gospel Writers forty years ago, the current arrangements of "Gospel Writer Boys Are We" (the group's theme song) and "Blind Bartamus" are virtually unchanged. Much the same can be said of the songs performed by the Royal Harmony Four and the Harps of Melody, for they, too, include many familiar spirituals like "Roll, Jordan, Roll" and "Old Time Religion." In short, these four groups maintain repertoires that fairly accurately reflect the style of singing widely performed in Memphis prior to the addition of musical instruments to quartets after World War II.

The best way to hear and appreciate this music is to experience it "live" and in the context of a rehearsal or church program. Since this is not possible for all but the most ardent fans and scholars, I will describe some of the music's most important traits using recorded examples as a guide.[10] These examples are listed in the Discography at the end of the book, and many are readily available on commercial records issued on the High Water label.[11]

All but one of the 1928–30 I. C. Glee Club recordings and the recent selections by the Gospel Writers, the Harps of Melody, and the Harmonizers are sung without instrumental accompaniment. The meter is almost always duple, either in 2/4 or 4/4, which is true of most prewar-style quartet recordings in Memphis. The only exception occurs when the ensemble momentarily drops out and the lead singer is left to improvise more spontaneously. In these unusual instances, such as the Harmonizers' "Trampin'" or the Gospel Writers' "Up above My Head I Hear Music in the Air," the meter is somewhat freer. The tonality is overwhelmingly major, the only exception among these groups being the Gospel Writers' "Wade in the Water," which is clearly derived from a 1950s recording by the Harmonizing Four of Richmond, Virginia (the earlier version is also performed in a minor key).

Four-part harmony consisting of alto, tenor, baritone, and bass is heavily stressed in this music. On rare occasions the group leaves the leader on his own or the singers alter their parts to form a three-part harmony, which is accomplished by "doubling" on one voice. One of the finest examples of four-part harmony is heard on the Harmonizers' showcase piece, "Roll, Jordan, Roll." Crossing of the inner voices also is fairly common, as in the final chord of the Harmonizers' "I'm Leaning on the Everlasting Arms." During this sustained chord the alto (lead) and tenor voices cross one another to end on the same note. This type of crossing results in parallel octaves, but it can often produce parallel fifths.

Quartets sometimes include more than four singers, in which case one is featured as a lead or two voices double on a single part. The Gospel Writers use a lead singer on "New Born Soul" and "I'll Fly Away"; their "Meet Me in Gloryland," which essentially has two tenor singers, offers another instance of doubling. Most quartets include a well-developed bass part, often interpolating a line distinct from the other voices; in fact, a pronounced bass is one of the most distinctive features of prewar Memphis quartets. One has but to listen to the chorus of "Riding on the Seminole" by the I. C. Glee Club, "Sing and Make Melody unto the Lord" by the Harps of Melody, or the final chorus of the Harmonizers' "My Lord Is Writing" to recognize the importance of this voice.

The lead singer and chorus are generally kept separate in quartet music, and it is quite clear which singer has the preeminent role. But on several songs, such as "I Am a Pilgrim and a Stranger," by the Harmonizers, overlapping does occur. The texture is usually homophonic, although simple polyphony is sometimes heard, and there is generally little melodic independence in the four parts sung by these groups. Extreme examples of this are "Steal Away," by the Harmonizers, and the I. C. Glee Club's "Come On, Don't You Want to Go?" Simple polyphony is evident on the I. C. Glee Club's rendition of "When They Ring Dem Golden Bells."

The mid- to late 1930s witnessed the beginning of a transition in Memphis's gospel quartet music from a primarily folk expression to a popular one. An element critical to this intermediary stage was the increasing number of out-of-town quartets appearing in Memphis. Many nonprofessional quartets had visited the city for church programs as early as the mid-1930s. Elijah Jones recalls that the True Loving Five from Little Rock, Arkansas, and the Lonesome Moaners of Hot Springs, Arkansas, appeared at the Columbus (Street) Baptist Church about 1933.[12] Such groups usually made two appearances—one on Saturday evening and the other on Sunday afternoon—with an admission charge of ten or fifteen cents per person to help defray the group's travel and other expenses. By the late 1930s, however, professional talent was coming to Memphis on a regular basis.

Local singers themselves helped to promote many out-of-town quartets, primarily because these Memphians were acquainted with the other singers. James Darling claims: "Well, I booked the first out-of-town groups into the city. The first group that came in was the Birmingham [Famous] Blue Jay Singers. That was before the Soul Stirrers came into Memphis. They were out on the road . . . [and] I booked them at the auditorium on Main Street."[13] Although the exact date of this program is not clear, it was no earlier than 1937 or 1938, which is when both the Soul Stirrers and the Famous Blue Jay Singers began touring full-time. Because it was the first such booking, Darling recalls it well:

> That was the first program we had for a dollar. All the programs before that had been twenty-five cents or fifty cents. This was the first major one. . . . Crump [the mayor of Memphis] had for some reason gave orders for colored and white not to mix at the show on Main Street. For that particular reason we couldn't have white people to attend this show. There was a whole lot of them wanted to come to the program, but he gave them orders not to come.[14]

Despite "Boss" Crump's intrusion, the first Memphis program by a professional black gospel quartet brought a large number of people into the auditorium. This success opened the gate for other groups interested in Memphis engagements. Within a year groups such as the Pilgrim Travelers and the Golden Gate Quartet were appearing in Memphis every few months. These professional programs had a profound influence on Memphis quartets, with perhaps the most significant being the realization that such musical religious events could be held outside the church for the singers' own profit. This was a critical change in perspective from the earlier attitudes about singing religious music for private gain. Although such a practice was unknown in Memphis as late as the middle 1930s, the first signs of private enterprise in quartet singing were quite evident by the late 1930s among local groups who brought in professional ensembles.

The performance style and general stage-image that professional groups presented signaled another important shift for Memphis quartets. Local harmony groups normally rendered programs in a very dignified and restrained manner. After all, their singing was part of a conservative Church of Christ, National and Progressive Baptist, or Methodist worship service and a reserved demeanor was appropriate in this context. Public appearances by them paralleled the groups' singing style, meaning suits or dresses appropriate for church or some other prominent social event.

Groups like the Famous Blue Jay Singers helped to change these customs, however, with their simple but expensive matched suits, known as "uniforms," and their dramatic stage presence. Where Memphis quartets once stood "flat-footed" and simply sang, these other groups began to move while performing, using hand gestures and vivid facial expressions to intensify the emotions expressed in their songs. Memphis groups soon incorporated these changes in performance style and dress so they would appear modern, progressive, and professional, and by the onset of World War II such innovations were widely embraced.

There were other signs, too, of professionalism among Memphis quartets. One was the expanding opportunities for groups to sing on local radio stations. By the 1950s all of the most important and influential local stations featured quartet singing, a phenomenon that was critical to the growth of the Memphis quartet tradition (see chapter 5). Black-owned and white-owned businesses observed the popularity of this music and began exploiting its commercial appeal by the late 1930s. One example of this was the co-sponsorship by the Littlejohn Taxi Company and Pate's Men's Shop of the Spirit of Memphis's radio broadcasts. The business community's interest in quartet singing also took other forms, as Theo Wade explains: "We used to sing for Wallace Johnson, the man who owned Holiday Inns. We used to sing for him up on the wagon beds; go to where he had houses. He used to call and tell us to send the group. He would send a truckbed and we would get up on the truckbed and sing for two hours. Of course, he would pay us, you know, for advertising his homes [for sale]. Some days we'd sell four or five houses for him!"[15] This tactic apparently proved successful, for Johnson later brought the Gospel Writers to Mississippi to help sell homes and churches there.

Not only were local groups more visible around Memphis, but they also began to perform throughout the Mid-South. The Spirit of Memphis, for instance, traveled to Birmingham, Alabama, as early as 1935 to appear on programs promoted by a Jefferson County entrepreneur named Puckett, who was to help the group with their initial recording. Other groups, like the Gospel Writers and the Four Stars of Harmony, also began expanding their audiences by traveling more often to Mississippi and western Tennessee on weekends. Clara Anderson, who helped organize and sang with the Golden Stars between 1938 and 1943, tells of her experiences:

> When we were with the Golden Stars, we were very young and we stayed out of town a whole lot. We would book programs . . . knew every cow path in between here and Birmingham! We'd go into the town . . . to the school and sing a couple songs. Then they'd give us dinner, [and we'd] get dressed up for the night's performance. We would stay there that particular night and get up the next morning . . . go on our way and go on to the next town. This wouldn't be more than fifty miles apart. Then it would be the same thing.[16]

At the time singers like Jethroe Bledsoe, Earl Malone, and Robert Reed of the Spirit of Memphis, Jack Franklin and James Harvey of the Southern Wonders, and Doris Jean Gary and Elizabeth Darling of the Songbirds of the South were all in their late teens or early twenties. Although these singers and their quartets were to become among the most influential Memphis groups, they began at an age when the new out-of-town quartets, with their fresh ideas, would have a lasting influence on them. "Jet" Bledsoe vividly recalls his earliest impression of a professional quartet: ". . . they were at the Manassas High School and we went to hear them. We had never seen a professional group with uniforms on, because we didn't sing with no uniforms! We just got out there and sang with what we had on. . . . so that's what kind of motivated us—the Blue Jays."[17]

Changes in singing style and physical appearance paved the way for the professional quartets, yet no Memphis group explored the possibility of singing for a living until the end of the 1940s. The

The Gold Stars in 1945: Mary Ruth Youngblood, Clara Anderson, Mary Louise Wilson, Hazel Cole, Sylvia Anne Garrett. *Courtesy of Clara Anderson.*

A Memphis neighborhood group, the Friendly Brothers Quartet, which was fronted by John and Robert Maddrie (second and third on the left) in the early 1940s. *Courtesy of Sylvia Smith.*

The Gospel Writers were one of Memphis's top groups in the late 1930s: (*top*) James Strong, Roy White, Elijah Jones; (*bottom*) James Joy, James Harvey. *Courtesy of Doug Seroff.*

In the mid-1940s the Southern Junior Girls sang in local churches. *Courtesy of Cleo Satterfield.*

The M. N. Gospel Singers began performing on WMPS radio about 1946: (*standing*) R. D. Rogers, Ozell Webster, Silas Hughes, Will Rodgers, Andrew Kelly, Nathaniel Breakenridge; (*seated*) Roosevelt Webster, Roosevelt Muse. *Author's collection.*

The True Friend Gospel Singers in 1946: Mose Walker, Louis Satterfield, Willie Gillon, R. C. Dixon. *Courtesy of Louis Satterfield.*

M and N Junior Girls about 1949: Virgy Kelly, Jesse Ruth, Willie Mae Gray, Cleo Satterfield, Elizabeth Kelly, Mildred Gage. *Courtesy of Cleo Satterfield.*

One of the best groups in north Memphis in the late 1930s was the Four Stars of Harmony: Edward O'Brian, Elijah Ruffin, Willie Partee, Demsy Harris. *Courtesy of Elijah Ruffin.*

The city's most famous group, the Spirit of Memphis, as they appeared about 1936: Freddie Johnson, Ramond Sanders, Hermon Paul, Lewis White, Robert Reed, Earl Malone, Jethroe Bledsoe. *Author's collection.*

The Spirit of Memphis, in 1948, about one year before the members became fulltime professionals: (*top*) Earl Malone, "Jet" Bledsoe; (*middle*) Theo Wade, James Darling; (*bottom*) Reverend Crenshaw, Robert Reed. *Courtesy of Cleo Satterfield.*

Quartet trainer and founder of the Gospel Writers, Elijah Jones, about 1945. *Courtesy of Doug Seroff.*

The Songbirds of the South, on the verge of turning professional in 1949: (*top*) Dorothy Murff, Elizabeth Darling; (*middle*) Julia Pruett; (*bottom*) Cassietta George. *Courtesy of Doug Seroff.*

The Famous Golden Stars

of Memphis, Tenn.

Presents Musical Recitals.

For Information write

Clara Mae Anderson, Pres and Mgr.
930 Woodlawn Street or
Phone 8-8381

Mary Louise Wilson, Secretary

Season's   Greatest   Attraction

Mr. J. A. Gray and His
FAMOUS LIVE WIRE SINGERS
Presents
THE FAMOUS GOLDEN STARS
Of Memphis Tenn

Sunday Aug. 25th, 1946   at 8:30 P M .
at the Carver House   3035 Bell Ave.

Advance $ 1;00   At Door $ 1-25

THE GOLDEN STARS AND MT. PISGUAH
GOSPEL SINGERS
..Presents The..
FAMOUS BARONS of HARMONY
GOSPEL SINGERS
Of Chicago Ill.
W. S. B. C. Radio Artists
Will Appear At The
PLEASANT GREEN M. B C,
Cor. Life and Nicholas St
Thursday Nite Aug. 2nd. 1945.   At 8:00 P . M.
Rev. J. M. Madison, Pastor

Admission, Adult--50c.

ATTENTION! THE FAMOUS

Golden Star Quartette
of Memphis, Tennessee, is presenting a
MUSICAL RECITAL
at the DUSABLE HIGH SCHOOL
SUNDAY. JULY 15th, 1945
Program Begins at 3:00 P. M.

Ticket $1.20

ATTENTION!
The Famous GOLDEN STAR QUARTET
Renowned Radio Artists of Memphis. Tenn. In a
Great Musical Program
WEDNESDAY EVENING, JULY 11th, 1945
at the Y. M. C. A., 1012 Maxwell Street
Program starts at 8:30 P. M.
There will also be other Great Gospel Singers appearing
on the same Program, so if you want to hear
good singing don't miss this gala event.
For Information Call MRS. CHRISTIAN—Canol 4378

Donation 75c

Tickets for performances by the Famous Golden Stars. *Author's collection.*

fact that it *could* be accomplished, however, was amply demon-strated ten years beforehand. Although commercialism in gospel quartet singing was becoming more and more evident, most Mem-phis ensembles continued singing only in their home churches and neighborhoods. A few groups began moving slowly toward the professional route, but most were not so inclined. According to Clara Anderson, who prior to forming the Golden Stars in 1938 sang with a community quartet, the Busyline Soft Singers:

> As a kid, we had a little neighborhood quartet. They just wanted to be busy in religious work and they called themselves the Busylines. We were a group dedicated to singing gospel songs and it didn't matter if we actually got anything out of it. We did a lot of singing during the week. We've played a lot of night programs, too. A lot of people told us we really should have gone professional, but we just liked singing and didn't want to go out for it.[18]

Many Memphis quartets apparently shared these feelings. Highly regarded groups, like the Royal Harmony Four, the M and N Sing-ers, and the Jolly Sunshine Boosters Club Quartet, occasionally sang outside of Memphis and the Mid-South, but their primary audi-ence was within the city. They supported the churches and con-gregations that had listened to and appreciated them over the years.

Despite such "unbusiness-like" motives, by 1941 Afro-American gospel music in Memphis and the rest of the country was inexora-bly moving toward professionalization. All of the key elements were present: a general, widespread interest in quartet singing, mass media support, a sense of commercial popularity, and the groups' willingness to travel for public appearances. This trend was stymied and virtually stopped by World War II, however. Gaso-line rationing greatly curtailed traveling for performance, and the war's virtual monopoly on materials and production shut down the record industry between mid-1942 and late 1943. Once the war ended, this music skyrocketed in popularity and Memphis was caught up in the fervor.

The Spirit of Memphis played an important role in popularizing and professionalizing quartet singing during the years following the close of the Second World War. Up through this stage of its career, the group was one of the most highly respected quartets in and around Memphis. During the war its members continued to travel to the surrounding states for weekend programs. When travel restrictions eased about 1945, they were eager to increase their out-of-town engagements, and James Darling rejoined the Spirit of Memphis to facilitate this:

> Well, I am the man that started them traveling. I [could] book them all over the country and that's one of the reasons that the Spirit of Memphis wanted me to take them over . . . the connections that I had across the country from booking my wife's group [the Song-birds of the South]. I finally agreed after Elizabeth talked me into it. I booked 'em with the Fairfield Four . . . [and] quite often with Mr. Harris in Detroit, the Shields Brothers in Cleveland, all those different groups.[19]

Darling added another significant facet to the group when alternating lead singers Silas Steele and Little Ax (Wilbur Broadnax) were brought into the fold. Darling recalls that Steele and Little Ax were fully blended into the group by early 1948:

> Silas Steele had talked with me long distance and told me that his fellows was getting old and not well. They couldn't go on the road anymore and he didn't know nothing but singing, had never did nothing else. He asked me if I thought I could get him with the Spirit of Memphis. . . . So I talked with the boys and they said yes. It was 'bout six months after that I got Little Ax, when we were in Pittsburgh. Bledsoe had done all the leading and I wanted to get him some help anyway . . . 'cause we were pretty hot at that time [with] "Days Past and Gone" and "Happy in the Service of the Lord." Those [songs] were really burning![20]

Steele had for many years been with the Famous Blue Jay Singers of Birmingham and was intimately acquainted with the hazards and benefits of full-time performing. The members of the Spirit of Memphis were quite willing to listen to him and to Darling and to learn from their vast experiences.

The Spirit of Memphis was now on the threshold of a major commercial and artistic breakthrough, but it could not quite break free of the confines of the Mid-South performance circuit it had worked for many years. Jethroe Bledsoe vividly recalls that the group journeyed throughout "Mississippi, Arkansas, Alabama, Knoxville . . . places like that. We didn't take it on as a job, professionally. We didn't go out professionally until Silas Steele got with us. At that time we were scared to go out there. We were liable to starve to death! Couldn't lose our jobs!"[21] The final, critical factor that pushed the group into the professional ranks was the release of their first commercial record, "I'm Happy in the Service of the Lord" / "My Life Is in His Hands" in the fall of 1949. Issued on the local Hallelujah label but almost immediately leased to De Luxe, this record had an immediate regional impact and provided the group members with all the impetus they needed to finally quit their extramusical jobs and go on the road.

The triumphs of the Spirit of Memphis were not lost on other local quartets. Perhaps the second most popular group was the Southern Wonders, who began singing in Memphis about 1942 as the Renowned Southern Wonders—a name that distinguished the group from a contemporary Blytheville, Arkansas, quartet named the Southern Wonders. The initial members of the group were Jack Franklin, James Harvey, Bill Jones, Andrew Black, and James Darling. True to the tradition, they began by singing in neighborhood churches and remained a popular, strictly local group for about ten years, during which they went through the standard maze of personnel changes. By 1950 the core of the group, which was soon to turn professional, was in place. According to Jack Franklin, the Southern Wonders' cofounder, ". . . it was after World War II that the later Southern Wonders were organized. It consisted of R. L. Weaver, Ernest McKinney, who is a pastor in town now, Artus Yancey, and Ernest Moore. L. T. Blair was our musicianer, our guitar player."[22]

As with the Spirit of Memphis, the key to the Southern Wonders' transition to a professional quartet was the addition of a single member, James Darling. Darling had been a founding member of the Southern Wonders but was enticed to rejoin the Spirit of Memphis in 1945. Due to a severe ulcer that limited his ability to travel, he decided to rejoin the Southern Wonders in 1952. Franklin credits Darling, with his vast number of professional contacts and his road savvy, as the primary force in guiding the Southern Wonders through its transition to a full-time touring quartet. By 1953 a fully recovered James Darling was providing invaluable assistance in booking programs, setting up the group's itinerary, organizing finances, and utilizing his network of professional contacts.

Some interesting parallels between the careers of these two

groups illustrate the changes in Memphis quartet singing. Both began as community or church-affiliated quartets whose traveling for performance increased just after the end of the war. The critical factor in each group's decision to turn professional was the addition of a member with extensive experience, who joined at a time when the general musical climate was favorable toward black harmony singing.

The interest local radio stations displayed in quartet singing also increased during the postwar era. Because the number of local quartets performing regularly on Memphis radio was quite substantial, they served to strengthen the music's popularity throughout the Mid-South. "Jet" Bledsoe recalls: "It surprised me . . . how the group kicked off because I didn't think we'd ever get twenty miles out of town to be booked. 'Course the radio stations helped a lot. When WDIA went 50,000 watts [in July 1954] that's what blew the top! We were getting letters from all over, far as the station would reach."[23]

All of these factors encouraged a third group, the Sunset Travelers, to join the Southern Wonders and the Spirit of Memphis on the professional circuit. Formed in 1950 by Grover Blake, the Sunset Travelers performed throughout the Mid-South for about three years before carefully moving up to professional status. Blake himself was highly motivated to make this change and had a very clear idea of what he wanted from his music:

> We [Blake and a friend] tried to get with other groups when we came here [from Mississippi in 1945], groups such as the Spiritual Four. They wanted us to go like other groups. I never wanted to sing like no other group. . . . they wanted us to mock the Pilgrim Travelers . . . but I didn't want to do that.
> . . . during that time, the music the people liked was the CBS Trumpeteers. They was real hot at that type of singing. Our singing was somewhat based like that. . . . There's just one group that I admired down through the years, and we may sound somewhat like that group, and that's the Dixie Hummingbirds.[24]

These statements reflect Blake's attitudes toward quartet singing as well as his own involvement with music, which was rooted in an extremely religious upbringing. He proved very capable at forming a strong quartet with popular appeal, a unique musical personality, and then taking it on the road full-time. Furthermore, Blake was a shrewd businessman, always willing to exploit the personal contacts he made with the out-of-town groups performing in Memphis: "We started dealing with the Sensational Nightingales and different groups like that. Then we began to move! Like the Traveling Echoes, they carried us all over the country and we took up with them. They carried us places we didn't know about!"[25] By the middle 1950s his numerous contacts and his business acumen earned the Sunset Travelers a recording contract with Don Robey's Duke label and a spot among the other professional quartets. The group's success places it alongside Detroit's Violinaires or Chicago's Kelly Brothers as second-echelon groups whose members made a comfortable living as singers but were never as popular as the Fairfield Four from Nashville or the Harmonizing Four of Richmond, Virginia.

The Spirit of Memphis, the Southern Wonders, and the Sunset Travelers toured at a time when many quartets were working the same basic circuit of cities and towns. Because of its strategic location and size, Memphis had its share of programs by traveling gospel quartets. Local quartets, particularly the Spirit of Memphis, "sponsored" (booked and promoted) many of these programs. These events most often featured at least one headline group, such as the Highway QCs, the Pilgrim Travelers, or the Caravans, who were supported by three or four other local or regional ensembles. The programs were most frequently held in the Mason's Temple, a 7,000-seat facility located just off Crump Boulevard in southwestern Memphis. Countless gospel music extravaganzas were held there throughout the 1950s, as fans packed into the building to listen to and applaud their favorite groups. According to announcements that appeared in the *Memphis World* and the *Tri-State Defender,* there was a major concert in this facility about every two months.

The Spirit of Memphis's manager through the 1950s, Jethroe Bledsoe, recounts a few of the "packages" he assisted in arranging: "When they started booking four professional groups together, I'm the one that put them together. [I] got a bus. That's what made the song battle, that's what started it. . . . We went all down in California, everywhere—the Soul Stirrers, Pilgrim Travelers, and the Swan Silvertones."[26] These kinds of tours quickly became very popular and were a standard feature of gospel programs by the early 1950s. People loved hearing all of the exciting groups in the demanding, high-tension atmosphere created by "song battles." Such battles pitted popular quartets in head-to-head competition, which was intensified by having the crowd's applause determine the winner.

During this period of frequent tours and competitions, the singers enjoyed a high status within the black community. Quartet programs were very popular, generating thousands of dollars in revenues. Quartet singers in the highest paid professional ranks, like the Spirit of Memphis, commanded weekly salaries of as much as $200, which meant it was possible to perform religious music *and* have a substantial income. The lure of glamour and financial well-being proved strong, and many local Memphis singers were encouraged to pursue careers with professional gospel quartets.

Another reason for the rapidly burgeoning popularity of quartet singing in Memphis during the 1950s was the music's increased documentation on commercial recordings. Although they do not provide a complete picture, these aural documents illustrate the important transformation that occurred in Memphis gospel quartet singing between the middle 1930s and the middle 1950s. One dramatic aspect of quartet singing that changed was that of repertoire. Most of the material sung by the early quartets consisted of either traditional songs or original songs cast in traditional formats. This canon remained an important component of postwar quartets but was augmented by an ever-growing number of composed gospel songs. For example, of the ninety-four songs recorded commercially by the Spirit of Memphis, the Southern Wonders, the Sunset Travelers, and the Brewsteraires during the 1950s, approximately one-half are newly composed. The rest of their recorded repertoires consists of more traditional or traditional-sounding songs, such as "Wish I Was in Heaven Sitting Down," "On the Battlefield," and "Take Your Burden to the Lord."

The addition of composed gospel songs is not surprising given their increased popularity among blacks and whites in the 1940s. Thomas A. Dorsey's "Precious Lord" and "Peace in the Valley" proved enormously popular. Two other prominent Afro-American gospel composers, Rev. W. Herbert Brewster and Lucie E. Campbell, were Memphians,[27] and both were active as songwriters during the second two decades of gospel music—1940 through 1960. At least two of Reverend Brewster's songs, "Move On Up a Little Higher" (1946) and "Surely God Is Able" (1950), have become gospel standards, while another, "Old Landmark" (1948) remains popular in Memphis. Campbell was not as prolific as Brewster, although "Just to Behold His Face" (1951) is still widely performed. With two such important composers in their own city, it was hardly surprising that Memphis quartets fortunate enough to record during the postwar boom readily incorporated into their repertoires these and other composed gospel songs. (In fact, the title of this book is derived from "I Am Happy in the Service of the Lord," written in 1945 by Faye Ernestine Brown and made popular by the Spirit of Memphis.)

Although it is evident that newly authored gospel songs were an integral part of the repertoires of postwar Memphis quartets, ascribing their authorship is problematic. Some of them, such as Roberta Martin's "Swing Down, Chariot" (1956), are unquestionably based on traditional themes. At least one song title, "I'm Going to Move On Up a Little Higher" is credited to more than one author—Reverend Brewster and Kenneth Morris—though Memphis groups generally sing the Brewster composition. Finally, there is no comprehensive resource book to check such credits. (The songs for which authorship is known are cited here with the publication date and sometimes the author's name.[28])

Memphis's black gospel quartets were quite different in 1950 from the I. C. Glee Club that traveled to New York to record its songs. "Cold War" doldrums may have settled across the country, but quartets soon helped to ignite the atmosphere with their flashy suits, exciting choreography, and extravagant programs. The singing itself changed as the groups kept up with current trends. For example, most groups now use some instrumental accompaniment, although each group performs at least a few a cappella numbers, such as the Southern Wonders' "Come Over Here," or "Just to Behold His Face" by the Spirit of Memphis. Quartets commonly are accompanied on guitar, and they also make use of drums and piano.

The role of the bass singer has lost some of its importance in black gospel quartet singing. Most groups deemphasized strong bass singers and prominent parts for bass singers during the 1950s, augmenting or replacing them with guitars. The bass singer is still important, though, for a cappella numbers and up-tempo "jubilee" songs such as the Spirit of Memphis's "Working til the Day Is Done," or "Wish I Was in Heaven Sitting Down" by the Sunset Travelers. These songs highlight "pumping" bass singing that is often syncopated, very percussive, and quite striking.

Tonality now is primarily major, although minor keys are occasionally heard. Two exceptions are "Storm of Life" and "Blessed Are the Dead" by the Spirit of Memphis. There are also a few instances in which a song modulates between major and minor keys: for example, "Let My People Go" by the Sons of Jehovah. The prewar duple meter continues to predominate, but two new time signatures, 12/8 and 6/8, are now often used. This so-called gospel meter began to be heard in all types of black American gospel music throughout the 1940s. An example among the "modern" Memphis quartets is the Pattersonaire's "Surely, God Is Able," one of the earliest popular gospel songs regularly performed in 12/8 time.

Background (or chorus) singing most often consists of four-part harmony, though sometimes there are only three distinctive parts, as in the Sunset Travelers' "I Am Building a Home" and the Brewsteraire's "Jasper Walls" (Rev. W. Herbert Brewster, 1953). The predominant four-part harmony consists of bass, alto, and two tenor voices, and the background singers often utilize percussive techniques during the chorus. One of the most noticeable elements of Memphis quartet singing from the 1950s is the use of these percussive effects, which heighten the rhythmic interest and tension. Willie Johnson of the Golden Gate Quartet pioneered this singing technique, which was adopted by Memphis singers. Earl Malone and Robert Reed (from the Spirit of Memphis) use some of the following techniques on their recordings: syncopated phrasing; repetitive, clipped, single syllable words; and emphasized, explosive vowels. Their versions of the "Swing Down, Chariot" and "Working til the Day Is Done" illustrate these techniques, as does the Sunset Travelers' "Traveling Shoes."

Among gospel quartets there is an increased emphasis on lead singing, possibly due to the importance of solo singers like Sister Rosetta Tharpe and Mahalia Jackson during the 1940s. By the 1950s Memphis quartets featured more singing by a designated lead singer, and most groups had more than one lead singer who alternated the lead or was featured on a specific number. For example, the Southern Wonders' ten Peacock sides spotlight three different lead singers: James Darling, R. L. Weaver, and Sammie Dortch. Both lead and background singers also more frequently use improvisatory techniques, one of the cornerstones of local quartet singing during this period being its highly ornamented style. Lead singers such as Silas Steele, Jethroe Bledsoe (the Spirit of Memphis) and O. V. Wright (the Sunset Travelers) utilize melismatic, falsetto, and sforzando vocal techniques to heighten the emotional impact of a song. Bledsoe's vocal on "Lord Jesus" provides a striking example of this, as does Wright's singing on "Lazarus."

Most instances of overlap occur between the leader and the chorus, a stylistic trait that has become common among black quartets. Perhaps the most important reason for this was the increased emphasis placed on improvisatory lead singing. This type of vocal arrangement usually means that the lead singer's improvisation carries over into the chorus, as in the Southern Wonders' "As an Eagle Stirrith Her Nest." The song structure of these groups also tends to be more repetitive, which facilitates lead singing. Memphis quartets of this period most often used an ABABAB format. The A section is the chorus, which is generally quite stable, while the B section is usually an improvised lead. Singers sometimes refer to the B section as the part where the lead singer can "stretch out" and display his or her arsenal of vocal approaches and tricks. The Spirit of Memphis typifies this structure in "If Jesus Had to Pray (What about Me)."

While only three Memphis quartets operated as full-time groups, there were perhaps a half-dozen others striving to attain this status. Although none of them reached their goal, they were able to capitalize on the widespread popularity of this music. Almost any group with a good sense of organization, a willingness to promote itself, and at least a modicum of talent could make money arranging local programs. These semiprofessional quartets were willing to trek as far as Chicago or Dallas for a weekend and then return to Memphis in time for work on Monday morning.

One man who belonged in this category is Julius Readers, who came to Memphis from nearby Clarksdale, Mississippi, in 1949 and quickly immersed himself in the burgeoning quartet scene. He became a singer and manager for the Spiritual Travelers between

1953 and 1958. Like a cadre of Memphis quartets that included the Sons of Jehovah, the Dixie Nightingales, the Gableaires, the Jubilee Hummingbirds, and the Jones Brothers, the Spiritual Travelers had professional aspirations; they just were never able to make it to the top. Readers recalls:

> The Gabelaires and the Jubilee Hummingbirds was my favorite groups to work with. At that particular time, the Jubilee Hummingbirds . . . were working under the name of the Harmony Echo. We traveled every weekend. We did a lot of stuff in Little Rock, St. Louis, and Chicago. We didn't do no daily shows, just weekends. We have been as far away as Dallas, Texas, [or] New Orleans and back for a weekend. We traveled some long trips and we mostly lose every Monday [from work].
>
> I had to go out and set up the engagements. Go from town to town, get sponsors to work with you on programs. Actually you were some like "meat and bread"; if you don't make no money to pay them, then automatically they didn't make no money.[29]

Instead of working with major groups in these large cities, Readers and others worked with the local semiprofessional quartets, setting up programs in large churches or small auditoriums. These bookings constituted a circuit that paralleled quartets. Those programs featuring semiprofessional quartets were held only on weekends because the singers had to maintain their regular jobs in order to support their families. Thus, Readers and his peers directed much of their energy toward securing engagements in churches near or in the larger towns scattered throughout the Mid-South.

> Back in the '50s . . . quartets were very popular. We could draw about as many people as any pastor could draw at his church on Sunday morning because people used to go out and hear quartet singers. We did stuff around Blytheville, Arkansas; Portageville, Missouri; Jackson, Tennessee. That was the backbone of gospel singing. [Programs were held] on Saturday afternoon, [again] at 7:30 P.M. and then again Sunday afternoon. Then we do a Sunday night. A lot of times we do four—Friday, Saturday, and Sunday, double on Sunday. We only sung at home maybe once or twice every ninety days.[30]

What separated these groups from the professional quartets probably had as much to do with good fortune, contacts, and karma as anything else. The Spiritual Pilgrims, the Jordan Wonders, and others had almost everything going for them: a strong desire for professional status, contacts with professional quartets and promoters, the ambition to work toward that goal, and a knowledge of how the booking system worked. They possibly lacked some of the inherent singing ability and polish possessed by their professional counterparts, but without aural evidence this remains a supposition. Readers assesses the situation this way: "The only reason we didn't go professional . . . we couldn't get on a professional [record] label. That's what held us back. We had the professional contacts. We had the guys with intention of being professional. They sung professional and they were respected as professional singers . . . but they never could get on the right track to be on a national label."[31]

Readers's viewpoint certainly has merit. Despite the number of recordings made by Memphis groups during the late 1940s and 1950s, not every worthy group had the opportunity to get into the studios. Whether or not this inhibited the careers of certain groups is very difficult to verify, yet it is almost certainly true that the lack of recording exposure denied them did not help. However, the ambiguous status experienced by so many of these semiprofessional ensembles in no way diminishes their substantial niche in history. They represented the dreams of many singers who aspired to be part of "name" groups at a time when black gospel music was both commercially prosperous and a respected expression of Afro-American religious culture. If nothing else singers like Readers, Frank Perkins of the Sons of Jehovah, and Doris Jean Gary of the Songbirds of the South were able to perform music they loved, see places they may never have seen otherwise, as well as sing on the same bill as the Dixie Hummingbirds or some other out-of-town professional group.

The increased popularity and commercialization of quartets signaled other changes in performance style and the stage presence of local groups. Along with the increased emphasis on theatrics came another dramatic element, the "sermonette." This is an emotional narration that accompanies a gospel song, either as a prologue or during the course of the performance itself. Sermonettes, a direct outgrowth of the biblical stories that were so important to the jubilee quartets, were often performed as *cante-fables* and had a stirring impact on the audience. Out-of-town groups introduced these sermonettes to Memphis quartets during the late 1940s. Silas Steele, who helped pioneer their use, popularized them within the city, as Earl Malone of the Spirit of Memphis attests:

> What can I say about Silas Steele . . . he was beyond compare! He was inspirational to a lot of lead singers. He brought out a style that nobody had and they capitalized on what he did singing. [Steele was known for] narrating through a song and the different lead singers picked up on that style. They started doing it, but Silas Steele was the first to sing a song and just narrate through with that inspirational feeling.[32]

This style quickly proved popular on records, too. One of the Spirit of Memphis's best-selling discs is "Lord Jesus," a sermonette recorded live at the Mason's Temple in 1952 which literally pulsates with a fervor that would have been impossible to replicate in a studio.

Despite the numerous steps taken by many Memphis quartets toward a popular base and away from their folk roots, these trends were not all-pervasive. Throughout the postwar years there was a vital and active grassroots movement that supported the more traditional quartets. For each of the professional and semiprofessional ensembles mentioned in this chapter, there were many more community-based quartets active in the city. Without exception, all of the professional singers in Memphis began performing in community or church quartets and moved on only when they could grasp an opportunity to shift and attain a different realm of musical worship. But most of the quartets in Memphis remained firmly rooted within the communities or churches that spawned them. The principal interests of groups like the Harps of Melody, the Evening Doves, and the Majestic Soft Singers were their musical ministry and the people they could reach in Memphis. These groups also have tended to endure over many years, providing musical and spiritual sustenance for their peers.

By 1960 quartet singing in Memphis had lost much of its popular support base, a shift in interest that was not unique to Memphis (see chap. 1). Popular music and culture are by definition ephemeral, and it was only a matter of time before interest in gospel harmony singing had to wane. For more than a decade, though, quartet singing proved to be one of the most favored forms of music in Memphis's black community. Why, then, did it suffer such an immense diminution in popularity? Perhaps the simplest and most direct answer is overexposure. There were literally dozens of quartets performing in Memphis following World War II. Appearances by touring groups at the City Auditorium or the Mason's Temple every six or eight weeks augmented the weekly singing of local quartets. If one considers the number of opportunities offered Memphians to hear this music "live" and adds to that the regularly scheduled radio broadcasts and availability of commercial phonograph records by quartets, it quickly becomes clear how quartet music saturated the market. Because quartet singing was immensely popular for so many years, artists like Jethroe Bledsoe have only come to understand in retrospect that "after a while they went to running it into the ground. That's what it was, too much!"[33]

While it is indisputable that the popularity of this music was inherently ephemeral and that quartets eventually suffered from overexposure, the increasing secularization that pervaded every phase of black gospel music is another strong reason for its decline.[34] Quartet singing began as a community event, but by the 1950s it had often moved away from its original context. Professionally promoted programs were frequently held in secular settings that drew thousands of enthusiasts who paid an admission fee. Such trends proved very distressing to some Memphians, who felt that gospel quartets had left their ideals behind. Such sentiments became stronger among the conservative members of the Afro-American religious community as this music grew in popularity. Harry Winfield, a former gospel pianist who played on many religious programs during the 1950s, articulates the concerns of the more conservative churchgoers:

The gospel during those early 1950s . . . [was] traveling more and more towards rock and roll music. They were changing their style and they were dancing on stage. They were now, more or less, giving performances. They were now walking on benches and getting sort of ridiculous. Quartet singers were now processing their hair and riding in Cadillacs, doing very much of the things that the gospel people attributed to the world, you know, drinking. We see you now on stage, can't hardly stand. The support they were formerly

getting from many people . . . was church people. They felt they
were being deceived. . . . lot of things happened that started people
totally against what was happening in the gospel field, as far as quartet was concerned.[35]

Winfield's points are incisive and well taken. By 1960 gospel
quartet music had drifted far from its sacred roots and into a decid-
edly secular world. Programs highlighted by touring professional
quartets entertained and diverted as much as they delivered a religious message. This treatment of religious music eventually turned
many stalwart churchgoers from quartets toward different forms of
gospel music. One type featured soloists, who were beginning to
regain some of the prominence they had lost following World War
II. Singers like "Professor" Alex Bradford, Bessie Griffen, Mahalia
Jackson, and Memphis's own Queen C. Anderson are just four solo
performers whose careers prospered during the middle 1950s and
into the 1960s. Another popular genre was the ensemble, such as
the Caravans and the Clara Ward Singers, which featured six or
eight singers accompanied by a keyboard player or a rhythm section. In Memphis, the Brewster Singers, who were named for Rev.
W. Herbert Brewster, reigned supreme.

By the late 1950s many of the harmony quartets from across the
nation found that they could no longer support themselves by
touring. The situation in Memphis once more mirrored trends outside the Mid-South. The Southern Wonders, wracked by personal
problems and conflicts, were on the road for five years before giving up in 1957. In 1960 "Jet" Bledsoe pulled the Spirit of Memphis
off the road, while the Sunset Travelers managed to scrape by until
1962. But despite the dramatic decline in its general popularity,
Afro-American gospel quartet singing in Memphis is by no means
moribund. At least a half-dozen older-style quartets still sing in
churches throughout the city, some of them, such as the Willing
Four Soft Singers and the Harps of Melody, having served their community for more than thirty years. Both the Spirit of Memphis and
the Royal Harmony Four have moved beyond the fifty-year mark.

Several other groups popular in the 1950s, most notably the Jubilee Hummingbirds, the Dixie Wonders, and the Southern Jubilees, no longer emphasize harmony singing and perform more
contemporary gospel tunes to the accompaniment of a full rhythm
section. These groups enjoy a greater following than do the older

harmony quartets because they have made a conscious effort to keep up with current trends in gospel music. Both the Jubilee Hummingbirds and the Dixie Wonders still perform "live" every Sunday over WDIA, and until 1980 the Jubilee Hummingbirds also had a weekly half-hour television show over WREG in Memphis. Although none of the current Memphis groups have recorded on a label of national prominence, many of them have issued recordings on local labels like Designer and Philwood.

Although the quartet harmony style may be out of vogue, there are several noteworthy examples of older singers who have deliberately formed new quartets to perpetuate prewar styles: the Harmonizers, founded by Elijah Ruffin in 1976; the revamped Gospel Writers, revived by their founder, Elijah Jones, in 1977; and two female groups, the Vance Ensemble and the Holy Ghost Spirituals, established in 1978 and 1979, respectively. In 1987 George Rooks organized the New Gospel Writers, choosing the name to honor his mentor. Community churches in Memphis still strongly support such groups, each of which performs regularly. The fact that these contemporary quartets sing almost exclusively in churches throughout the city helps to underscore the fact that this music has gone full circle—from its folk roots to the popular realm and back again. Above all, the cultural and musical history of Memphis gospel quartets directly relates to this grassroots support and its unique community of singers—a concept to be explored in chapter 4.

NOTES

1. Personal correspondence, Robert O'Brien to Kip Lornell, July 27, 1982.

2. Haywood Gaines, interviewed by Kip Lornell, June 24, 1982. Unless indicated otherwise, all interviews were conducted by the author in Memphis, Tennessee. Transcript copies and tapes are on deposit at the Mississippi Valley Collection, Brister Library, Memphis State University.

3. Ibid.

4. Frank Miller, interviewed via telephone from St. Louis, Missouri, August 8, 1982.

5. Theo Wade, interview, October 1979.

6. James Darling, interviewed via telephone from Los Angeles, California, July 21, 1982.

7. Ibid.

8. Norman Cohen, *Long Steel Rail* (Urbana: University of Illinois Press, 1983), cites examples of these images, as do the contemporaneous recorded sermons by Afro-American preachers such as Rev. J. M. Gates and Rev. J. C. Burnett.

9. These older spirituals appear in the following collections: William Allen et al., *Slave Songs of the United States* (1867; rpt., New York: Oak Publishers, 1965) and J. B. T. Marsh, *The Story of the Jubilee Singers* (Cleveland: Cleveland Printing and Publishing, n.d.).

10. Some scholars would argue for the use of Western notation to transcribe these selections. However, Mantle Hood, in *The Ethnomusicologist* (Kent, Ohio: Kent State University Press, 1984), pp. 50–123, carefully points out the general limitations of this system.

11. The specific problems inherent in using this approach in transcribing Afro-American gospel music are noted by William Tallmadge, brochure notes, *Jubilee to Gospel—A Selection of Commercially Recorded Black Religious Music, 1921–1953*, JEMF-108 (Los Angeles, 1980), pp. 7–8. The descriptive system used here is similar to that employed by George Herzog, "The Yuman Musical Style," *Journal of American Folklore*, 41 (1928), pp. 183–231; and George Ricks, *Some Aspects of the Religious Music of the United States Negro* (New York: Arno Press, 1978).

12. Elijah Jones, interview, October 1979.

13. Darling interview.

14. Ibid.

15. Wade interview.

16. Clara Anderson, interview, April 18, 1982.

17. Jethroe Bledsoe, interview, January 21, 1981.

18. Anderson interview.

19. James Darling, interview, August 2, 1983.

20. Ibid.

21. Bledsoe interview.

22. Jack Franklin, interview, June 21, 1980.

23. Bledsoe interview.

24. Grover Blake, interview, July 10, 1982.

25. Ibid.

26. Bledsoe interview.

27. For more information see Eileen Southern, "W. Herbert Brewster," p. 47, and "Lucie E. Campbell," p. 55, in *Biographical Dictionary of Afro-American and African Musicians* (Westport, Conn.: Greenwood Press, 1982).

28. The most important source for this information is Irene V. Jackson,

comp., *Afro-American Religious Music: A Bibliography and a Catalogue of Gospel Music* (Westport, Conn.: Greenwood Press, 1979).

29. Julius Readers, interview, May 28, 1982. For additional information on this strata of Memphis quartets see Hank Davis, "Sun's Jones Brothers," *Whiskey, Women, and . . . ,* no. 16 (Spring 1987), pp. 16, 17.

30. Ibid.

31. Ibid.

32. Earl Malone, interview, October 11, 1980.

33. Bledsoe interview.

34. Tony Heilbut, *The Gospel Sound—Good News and Bad Times* (New York: Simon and Schuster, 1984), pp. 281–307.

35. Harry Winfield, interview, July 14, 1982.

CHAPTER

3

"I've Got on My Traveling Shoes"

Black gospel quartet singers in Memphis have always been highly mobile, spreading their music throughout the Mid-South and beyond. This mobility has created unique patterns of movement that are of special interest to cultural geographers.[1] Most important, the singers have left their imprint on the spatial landscape by developing special travel patterns that were largely correlated to their degree of amateur or professional status. Secondarily, the names of gospel quartets, their song titles, and their lyrics reflect themes of environmental perception and sense of place.

The movement of people and the process itself is multifaceted because migration involves more than a simple shift from one geographical location to another. Nearly 85 percent of the approximately fifty Memphis gospel quartet singers I interviewed were born in the Mid-South; of the rest, nearly all moved from other parts of the South to Memphis as children. Virtually all of them relocated to Memphis directly from small towns or rural areas located within approximately one hundred miles of the city (Figure 1). The fact that Memphis was the final destination for these singers underscores its position as the most important urban center in the Mid-South. Somewhat surprisingly, none of the singers moved specifically to join a quartet, nor did any groups migrate en masse.

Avery Savage, founder in 1937 of the Zion Hill Spirituals, followed the typical pattern. Savage spent most of his childhood on his parents' farm in eastern Arkansas. In 1936 he moved to Osceola, Arkansas, but was not able to land a steady job and within a matter of months journeyed to Memphis in search of secure employment, which was quite elusive during the late days of the depression: "When I first got to Memphis, I worked for Q. S. Transfer Company. From there to Happy Feed Company. . . . after they ran low and laid off, I left . . . and went to Fisher Body Company. Fisher laid off and I went to Kelsy Wheel Company, shipping wheels. When they laid off, I went to Buckeye, which is a subsidiary of Procter and Gamble. That's when I hit it! I worked for them forty-one years and then retired."[2] Savage's experiences were echoed some ten years later by Robert Royston, of the Wells Spiritual Singers, who moved to Memphis from Holly Springs, Mississippi: "I had just gotten out of the service and felt I wanted to move from down there. There were better jobs [in Memphis]. . . . I wouldn't say they were so much better, but I *did* find work at the H. C. Taylor Company down there on Front Street. Finally I got a job down at the Defense Depot; been there ever since."[3]

Of the black gospel quartet singers who relocated to Memphis, most were primarily motivated by the harsh realities of a bleak rural economy. Attracted by a job market that at least offered blue-collar work, they generally arrived in Memphis with poor or non-existent educational backgrounds and eagerly accepted whatever work they could find. This was especially true throughout the 1930s, until World War II pulled the country out of the depression. Memphis also offered social and cultural amenities like restaurants, movie theaters, libraries, and night clubs. The pace of city life was generally quicker and more varied than in the settings from which these singers had come. As Elijah Ruffin, who moved to Memphis from Sardis, Mississippi, in 1929, states: "I always did like the city. . . . I just got tired of it down there [in Mississippi]!"[4] This simple observation articulates what many rural blacks probably felt and also indicates some of the "push" and "pull" factor for rural black migration into Memphis.[5] George Davis and Fred Donaldson, two geographers with an interest in migration patterns involving the rural South and northern cities, have paid special attention to black migration. They have observed that black Americans who moved from Arkansas, Mississippi, and Tennessee during the 1950s favored Chicago as a northern destination but that Mem-

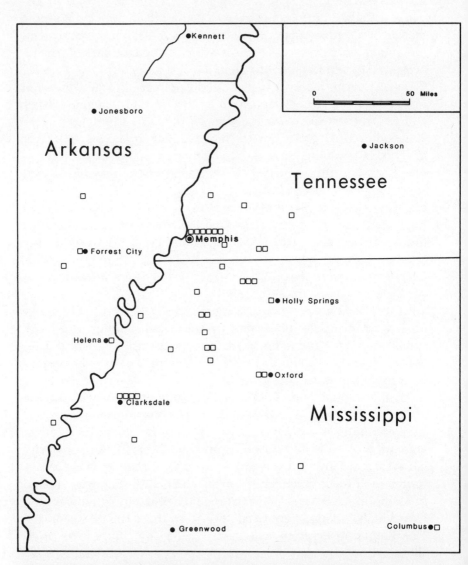

Figure 1 locates the birthplaces of thirty-nine of the Memphis gospel quartet singers interviewed. Most of these singers were born in small towns or rural hamlets located within 100 miles of Memphis. The spatial distribution underscores the importance of rural to urban migration, which later influenced performance travel patterns.

phis was the "important local destination" for this same group.[6] (The significance of this link between the rural and urban South and cities in the North for Memphis quartet singers will soon become apparent.)

While the migration of blacks and black quartet singers to Memphis almost always represented a permanent move, the routes they traveled for out-of-town performances have been predictably multidirectional and fall into two basic categories directly related to the group's professional, semiprofessional, or nonprofessional status. These categories also reflect the amount of travel and the time each group could devote to out-of-town engagements. All but about ten of the eighty documented groups that have performed in Memphis since the 1920s have been nonprofessional, and as such their travel patterns have generally been limited to the Mid-South. While the place names and precise locations of the small towns and rural communities differ, most Memphis gospel quartets have trod remarkably similar terrain over the past forty to fifty years. They seem to have sent representatives to almost every black church located within one hundred miles of the city.

Typical of such quartets active in Memphis during the 1940s and 1950s are the Southern Jubilees, the Zion Hill Spirituals, and the Orange Mound Specials. According to Floyd Wiley, the Southern Jubilees have given innumerable programs throughout the Mid-South, particularly in Mississippi, since 1938. Most of the performances have taken place on the weekends in small churches located in the Yazoo Basin (e.g., Rosedale, Beulah, and Shelby). At one time the group even performed in the "boot-heel" area of Missouri, singing in towns like Hayti and Saxon. However, these out-of-state trips became less frequent in the mid-1950s when the Southern Jubilees' popularity in Mississippi began to grow.

Similarly, the Zion Hill Spirituals, who represented the Zion Hill Baptist Church from 1939 until 1972, traveled a modest distance outside Memphis to sing. Unlike the Southern Jubilees, though, the Zion Hill Spirituals' performance territory included eastern Arkansas as far west as Little Rock. Most of the programs were held in the east quarter of that state, particularly around Osceola and Blytheville. The group occasionally performed in small towns in northwestern Mississippi and sometimes sang as far south as Greenwood, nearly one hundred miles south of Memphis.

The Orange Mound Specials existed from about 1936 until the outbreak of World War II. A former member, Elijah Ruffin, recalls that the group traveled in all directions from Memphis. In Arkansas they often performed in West Memphis, Forrest City, Brinkley, Blytheville and Osceola, while their Mississippi trips took them to Como, Mount Pleasant, and Holly Springs. Western Tennessee was also within their domain; they sometimes journeyed as far away as Jackson and Covington.

Figure 2 gives the general location of performances by the Golden Stars, the Harps of Melody, the Orange Mound Specials, the Zion Hill Spirituals, the Southern Jubilees, and the Spiritual Pilgrims between 1940 and 1955. A comparison of this figure and Figure 1 reveals a strong correlation between the birthplaces of quartet singers I interviewed and the locations of later performances of six of the most popular groups. The two maps clearly indicate that northwestern Mississippi was the favorite location for performances by nonprofessional quartet singers, which implies that directional biases are closely related to long-standing kinship-friendship ties with childhood communities.

Where a group traveled to perform often resulted from ongoing contacts in the singers' former homes. Indeed, the quartet performance network largely depended on friends and relatives who contacted various Memphis groups to request an appearance. These rural dwellers provided an extremely important emotional and musical link between country and city, creating a vital bond with the singers' childhoods and another aspect of "down-home" life that was probably experienced by every black Memphian who moved in from the country. Most of the Memphis singers eagerly anticipated the trips back to Mississippi because of the chance to see old friends and relatives and to feast on home cooking. In many ways these intangible networks were closely related to the migration patterns observed by Davis and Donaldson.[7]

Floyd Wiley, the first president of the Memphis chapter of the National Quartet Convention, describes how the quartet network functioned: "Sometimes we would have relatives or maybe another group down there. You might contact them or maybe they contact you and say they wanted to get you down there. Some days you might be up in Missouri and somebody from down in Mississippi might be visiting there and they hear you and contact

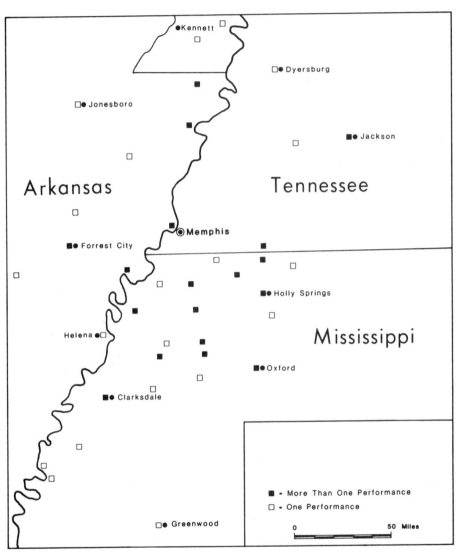

Figure 2 locates the sites at which the Golden Stars, the Harps of Melody, the Orange Mound Specials, the Southern Jubilees, the Zion Hill Spirituals, and the Spiritual Pilgrims performed between 1940 and 1950. Many gospel quartet singers performed in or near their places of birth, the result of kinship contacts and other networks that facilitated bookings for performances.

you."[8] Churches, schools, and small auditoriums provided the settings for most of these programs, which, as a general rule among most nonprofessional Memphis quartets, occurred once or twice a month. Longer trips outside the Mid-South usually took place only once or twice a year.

Since the late 1920s radio broadcasts have also affected this network. Beginning with the I. C. Glee Club in 1928 and continuing regularly through the early 1960s, quartets performed over the airwaves. People residing in rural areas wrote either to the quartets themselves or to the radio station, requesting that the singers appear at their local church or auditorium. Mary Davis of the Majestic Soft Singers recalls how this worked:

> From Memphis, Tennessee . . . down to Mississippi, far as you could go: Marks, Como, Hernando, Clarksdale. . . . All over Arkansas, I can't name all those little places—I done forgot. We went so many places! Every Sunday or so, we were gone. . . . At one time we was broadcasting [and] a lot of times they would say, "We heard you on the air." They would call me or write me a letter . . . ask us was we booked up for a certain time.[9]

The Songbirds of the South and the Dixie Nightingales, in particular, developed a significant following as a result of their radio broadcasts and subsequent personal appearances.

The social and musical kinship network also played an important part in the long-distance performance travel of quartets. Although groups like the Harmonizers and the Jolly Sunshine Boosters Club Quartet never sang outside the Mid-South, forty or fifty other Memphis quartets did travel longer distances. To a great extent these groups utilized the same networks that brought them to rural Arkansas, Mississippi, Tennessee, and Missouri. The primary difference in the networks is that these new routes followed the long-established migration routes from the South to cities in the North.

The Pattersonaires, for example, have been making regular pilgrimages to churches in the North since the middle 1950s. Their main contact was initially through the Reverend Charles J. Patterson, after whom the group is named. Reverend Patterson, now deceased, was a Baptist minister in Memphis before he moved to Lansing, Michigan, in 1955. For many years he booked the Pattersonaires in the Detroit area. Now the group makes an annual one-week to ten-day tour there each summer.

Another nonprofessional Memphis group, the Golden Stars, made regular trips north between 1940 and 1945. As Clara Anderson explains: "We went to Chicago on our own. One of the girls had some sisters in Chicago. . . . They were up in Chicago and they had a group . . . [and] booked us at DuSable High School and around in different churches. We even got our picture in the *Chicago Defender!*"[10] The Golden Stars also made trips to St. Louis, appearing on programs booked by friends who had moved there, thus extending the Memphis-area network.

Many other groups, including the Pilgrim Spirituals and the Campbellaires, made annual or semiannual journeys north during the 1940s and 1950s. Like the Golden Stars, these nonprofessional quartets usually sang on programs that former neighbors, friends, relatives, or other quartet singers who had permanently settled in cities like South Bend, Chicago, or Detroit had arranged. The groups made these trips over long weekends or during vacations in order not to lose time from work.

A different, though related, network developed for local semiprofessional and professional quartets—a status to which the overwhelming majority of quartets in Memphis neither aspired to nor achieved. Only the Spirit of Memphis, the Southern Wonders, and the Sunset Travelers worked as full-time quartets, while the semiprofessional ranks consisted of the Sons of Jehovah, the Dixie Nightingales, the Dixie Wonders, and the Spiritual Travelers. The three professional quartets spent much of the 1950s touring the country full-time—a level of commitment about which semiprofessional groups only dreamt.

Instead of a cadre of friends, relatives, and local groups, Memphis semiprofessional and professional groups relied upon a small number of booking agencies and some of the other touring quartets for most of their dates. This created radically different travel patterns from the majority of the other quartets in Memphis. Based on interviews with Grover Blake of the Sunset Travelers and Jack Franklin of the Southern Wonders, it is possible to reconstruct something of their performance itineraries. Grover Blake explains how he arranged extended tours: "Sometimes we'd book two or three months or some dates further than that. Just scattered dates, you know; then we'd try and fill in. After I learned about booking

. . . it's like if we leave here going to California, I'll book my way all the way from here into California. Then I'll book myself all the way out of California. If I go to New York, I'll book myself there and I'll book myself back."[11]

As for the routes themselves, Blake recounts a lengthy, meandering trip his group made about 1956:

> We came out of Key West and sang in Jacksonville, Pensacola, Mobile, Hattiesburg, New Orleans, Baton Rouge, Shreveport. Then we got into Dallas, next we go into Oklahoma. We leave Oklahoma, I think we sang in Kansas City. We come out of Kansas City and into Odessa and Amarillo, Texas. Then we sing in Albuquerque, New Mexico. Then into Phoenix, then into Los Angeles and into Bakersfield. We sang in White Springs, California; then we moved into Oakland. Then we sing in Reno, Nevada—into El Paso [and] in Houston.[12]

Such travel was wearing, tedious, and demanding. Quartet singers had to be dedicated to their careers and to singing, for as Blake explains, life on the road had many hardships along with the financial and spiritual rewards: ". . . you got to pay your dues on the road! There are times when the crowds are thin, but you still got to go on. Then you go places and sometimes your shows are cancelled when you get there. Then you move on and the next program is good. . . . You've got to have some guys who are willing to stick-up and follow what they believe."[13]

While the Sunset Travelers appeared on programs throughout the southern half of the United States, particularly in the Deep South and Southwest out to the West Coast, the Southern Wonders booked their engagements elsewhere. Most of their programs took place in the south-central states, and according to Jack Franklin, the Southern Wonders also were favorites in "Arkansas—Little Rock, Hot Springs, Pine Bluff, Hughes, Helena, Forrest City, and Mariana—and in Mississippi—Vicksburg, Natchez, Jackson, Grenada, Aberdeen, Ponotoc, Tupelo, Columbus, Indianola, Greensville, and Clarksdale. Great big cities!" he observed with a laugh.[14]

The Southern Wonders' dates were arranged through the Buffalo Booking Agency in Houston, Texas, home of their record label, Peacock Records. This agency, which also booked such important national artists as the Bells of Joy and the original Five Blind Boys, set up programs for the Southern Wonders in midwestern cities. Franklin recalls that they were booked into such places as

Racine, Wisconsin, Waterloo, Iowa, and Mayfield, Kentucky—not locations one would usually think of as critical performance points for black quartets. But professional quartets traveling in buses or automobiles often sang in many smaller cities because these dates helped to fill the gaps between the more lucrative programs in big cities.

The travel patterns of the local semiprofessional groups are even more difficult to establish. While these singers tended to perform in the Mid-South, they were often booked in more distant cities like Dallas and New Orleans. Julius Readers of the Spiritual Pilgrims recalls trekking to Chicago or Detroit every other month during the mid-1950s. Most of these trips were limited to weekends because the group members all held full-time jobs and sang partly to augment their incomes. Perhaps the wildest trip was made by the Jordan Wonders in about 1952 when they drove to Rochester, New York, for a single Saturday night engagement and were back in Memphis for work on Monday morning! The only quartet whose performance routes are possible to track precisely is the Spirit of Memphis. Jethroe Bledsoe, the group's business manager from the 1950s, kept a travel diary listing each place the quartet sang in during the spring and summer of 1952 (see Appendix II), at the apex of its commercial success. During the most favorable travel months—April through September—the quartet performed as far west as Oakland, California, and as far east as Newark, New Jersey (see Figure 3).

A large automobile or touring limousine was the usual mode of transportation for these groups. During the 1950s the Sunset Travelers owned four limousines and drove them all into the ground. The Spirit of Memphis toured so much between 1950 and 1955 that no group member can recall the number or model of cars they used. If the spring and summer 1952 itinerary is exemplary of their nationwide bookings for the early 1950s, then the Spirit of Memphis drove in excess of 50,000 miles each year, or at least half a million miles in one decade.

At first glance the travel patterns of Memphis quartet singers appear to be random, but they were clearly influenced by many underlying economic, cultural, and social factors, including group members' places of birth or who wrote for a quartet booking as the result of a radio broadcast. The patterns are also the result of choices, such as the groups' nonprofessional or professional status.

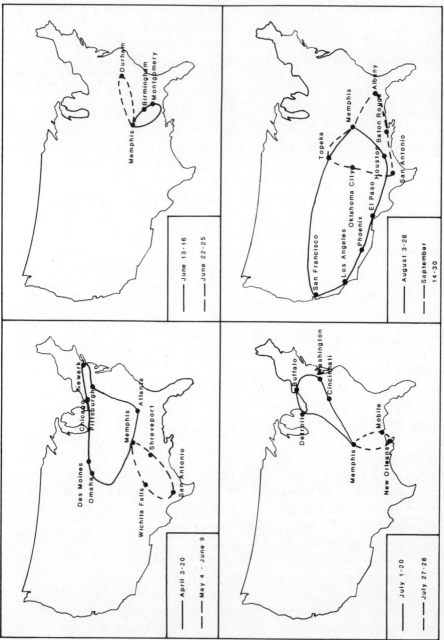

Figure 3 shows the travel patterns created by the Spirit of Memphis between April and September 1952. Derived from a diary kept by their manager, Jethroe Bledsoe, this map demonstrates the extent to which a popular professional group traveled during the height of interest in black gospel quartets.

Hence, the basic ingredients shaping these spatial patterns are of interest not only to geographers but to anyone seeking to understand the human factors related to music. It is also worth observing that geographical themes are significant to the spatial study of this type of music. Among Memphis groups two different components—names of quartets, and song titles and lyrics—underscore a subtle polarity. Simply stated, quartet names often reflect a real geographic location, while song titles and lyrics frequently maintain a more ethereal orientation. To fully explore this dichotomy it is necessary to look at the names that Memphis quartets have used over the past sixty years. These names function on at least three levels of geographic orientation, and all reveal important clues to the singers' sense of place.

Many groups in Memphis chose generic religious names such as the Four Kings of Harmony, the Pilgrim Spirituals, the Willing Four Soft Singers, the Christian Harmonizers, or the Sons of Jehovah. Significantly, other quartets selected monikers with definite geographic implications. On the most general level are names reflecting a regional orientation toward the South: the Songbirds of the South, the Southern Bells, the Southern Wonders, the Dixie Nightingales, the Dixie Wonders, the Southern Jubilees, and the Southern Harmony Boys. Other Memphis quartets' names clearly establish their sense of identity with that city, the most obvious example being the Spirit of Memphis. But at least two other groups, the Memphis Spiritual Four and the Delta Friendly Four of Memphis, also bear the city's name. On an even more specific level, other gospel quartets picked names referring to locations within Memphis. Some, such as the Orange Mound Specials, the North Memphis Harmonizers, the Magnolia Specials, and the Orange Mound Harmonizers, chose their names from readily identifiable neighborhoods or sections of the city. The most explicit example is the Wells Spirituals, whose members rehearsed on Wells Street.

Interestingly, many secular black groups in Memphis have used a similar naming system. Several important blues groups from the 1920s—the Beale Street Jug Band, the Beale Street Sheiks, and the Beale Street Rounders—openly identified with the city's best-known, most notorious street. Two other noted blues singers, Minnie McCoy and Peter Chatman, performed and recorded as Memphis Minnie and Memphis Slim, respectively. Finally, there was the loose, easy-going conglomeration of musicians called the Memphis

Jug Band, well known throughout the Mid-South during the 1920s and 1930s from their live performances and numerous recordings for the Victor and OKeh labels.

Of course, not all Memphis gospel musicians were so geographically inclined. Some groups adopted their employer's names, such as the various groups associated with the Illinois Central Railroad: the I. C. Glee Club, the I. C. Harmony Boys, and the I. C. Hummingbirds. This practice occurred because the workplace often served as a common meeting ground as well as a practice site. The Orval Brothers (Construction Company) Quartet was active during the late 1920s, and the Keystone Masters of Harmony took their name from the sponsor of their late-1940s radio broadcasts—the Keystone Beauty Products Company. Still other groups chose a more pedestrian path by selecting the name of their "home" church to represent their group. This resulted in quartets like the Middle Baptist Quartet, the Lake Grove (Baptist) Specials, the Mount Moriah (Baptist) Wonders, the T. M. and S. (Baptist) Quartet, and the M. and N. (Baptist) Singers. At least two other Memphis quartets chose the name of their spiritual leader: Rev. Charles J. Patterson inspired the Pattersonaires, while Rev. W. Herbert Brewster, a noted songwriter and pastor of the East Trigg Baptist Church, was similarly honored by the Brewsteraires and the Brewster Singers.

It is clear from these examples that a significant percentage of black gospel quartet names in Memphis reflect geographic alignments. In fact, of the eighty quartets listed in Appendix I, approximately 35 percent selected names that identified them directly with Memphis, and nearly 10 percent chose names that aligned them with the South (the remaining 55 percent displayed no apparent geographic sense of place). All of this underscores how often people identify with names that reflect a feeling of belonging and a spirit of pride in a specific place—a phenomenon not limited to black gospel quartets in Memphis, of course. For instance, state university nicknames like the University of Florida "Gators," the University of Nebraska "Cornhuskers," or the University of Maine "Bears" can evoke a strong response from fervent, loyal alumni, whose pride is reflected in such visible, public ways as bumper stickers, beer mugs, and sweatshirts.

Although the names of many Memphis gospel quartets suggest a definite worldly orientation, their songs often express a yearning to reach an ethereal realm—an abstract heaven rather than their present home. This opposition underscores the ambivalence many people feel toward mortality. Memphis quartet singers acknowledge these human limitations through group names and songs by simultaneously balancing the concept of heaven with earth's reality. Furthermore, it is just one more way in which these singers cope with the daily dilemma of how to reconcile their spiritual and worldly lives. This celestial inclination is most readily apparent in titles like "Wish I Was In Heaven Sitting Down" (the Sunset Travelers), "Home in the Sky" and "Automobile to Glory" (the Spirit of Memphis), "Highway to Heaven" (the Harmonizers), "Meet Me in Gloryland" (the Gospel Writers), "Heaven Is My Goal" (the Holy Ghost Spirituals), and "I Am Bound for the Promised Land" (the Harps of Melody). Such titles follow the strong Christian willingness to trade this life for a locale far removed from south Memphis, Orange Mound, Wells Street, or any other place on Earth.

Memphis quartet song lyrics often express similar sentiments. The Brewsteraires, for example, wish to "just move on up the King's highway" because "it's a highway that leads up to heaven"; the "King" refers, of course, to Jesus. Similarly, the I. C. Glee Club associates Memphis and heaven when it sings of the "ride home on the Chickasaw train." One of the most powerful and direct heaven-bound metaphors found in this corpus is "Milky White Way" by the Spirit of Memphis:

> Yes, I'm going to walk the milky white way,
> One of these old days.
> Gonna walk up and take my stand,
> Gonna join that Christian band,
> Woah, woah, one of these old days.

Metaphors, allusions, and related images of travel and movement are an important part of the language that quartet singers in Memphis use. These devices are also commonly found in other forms of Afro-American folk music, most notably in the blues.[15] Such similarities are not surprising in light of the important oral tradition and backgrounds shared by many blues and gospel singers.

Literary scholars have long applied the methods of textual analysis to poetry, short stories, and novels in order to gain a greater awareness of implicit cultural and personal values. Other scholars have used semiotics to understand the symbolism that underlies many everyday objects like the American flag. An analogue is the expensive, matched suits and ornate uniforms worn by the quartets which signify a deeper cultural, musical, and religious unity and dignity. From the geographer's perspective, a close examination of the names selected by these quartets and the songs they perform helps us to better understand the singers' often subconscious perceptions of their own environment.

NOTES

1. For a comprehensive, annotated bibliography of this scholarship see Kip Lornell, "Diffusion, Migration, and Sense of Place: The Geography of American Folk and Popular Music," *Current Musicology,* 37/8 (1984), pp. 127–35.

2. Avery Savage, interviewed by Kip Lornell, March 22, 1982. Unless indicated otherwise, all interviews were conducted in Memphis, Tennessee, by the author. Copies of the interview tapes and transcripts are deposited in the Mississippi Valley Collection, Brister Library, Memphis State University.

3. Robert Royston, interview, April 21, 1982.

4. Elijah Ruffin, interview, March 2, 1981.

5. Paul T. Bechtol discusses this phenomenon in "Migration and Economic Opportunities in Tennessee Counties" (Ph.D. dissertation, Vanderbilt University, 1962), pp. 81–102.

6. George O. Davis and Fred O. Donaldson, *Blacks in the United States: A Geographic Perspective* (Boston: Houghton Mifflin, 1975), p. 44.

7. Ibid., pp. 30–34.

8. Floyd Wiley, interview, March 15, 1982.

9. Mary Davis, interview, May 10, 1982.

10. Clara Anderson, interview, April 18, 1982.

11. Grover Blake, interview, July 10, 1982.

12. Ibid.

13. Ibid.

14. Jack Franklin, interview, May 31, 1982.

15. These scholars examine the language and lyrics of blues singers: Samuel Charters, *Poetry of the Blues* (New York: Oak Publications, 1963); Norm Cohen, *Long Steel Rail: The Railroad in American Folksong* (Urbana: University of Illinois Press, 1983); David Evans, *Big Road Blues: Creativity in the Folk Blues* (Berkeley: University of California Press, 1982); and Jeff Todd Titon, *Down Home Blues Lyrics* (Boston: G. K. Hall, 1982).

The Gospel Writer Junior Boys had achieved semiprofessional status by 1953: (*top*) Willie "Pop" Jones, Roy Neal, Willie Neal, Clyde Howard; (*bottom*) Ollie Hoskins, Willie Pettis, Thomas Caldwell. *Courtesy of Marie Walton.*

One of America's most popular quartets of the early 1950s, the Five Blind Boys of Mississippi. *Author's collection.*

Beginning in the late 1940s the Famous Pilgrim Travelers toured the country from their Los Angeles base. *Author's collection.*

By 1946 the Soul Stirrers had been an innovative and influential quartet for nearly a decade. *Courtesy of Cleo Satterfield.*

The Golden Gate Quartette, circa 1948, perhaps the single most re-spected quartet for two decades, beginning in 1937. *Author's collection.*

In 1952 the Sunset Travelers were about to enter the studios for Duke Records: (*top*) Lonnie Walton, Bill (?), Adam (?), Sam Miller; (*bottom*) McKinney Jones, Walter Pittman, Grover Blake. *Courtesy of Marie Walton.*

Beginning in 1949, thousands of Memphis residents tuned in to "Cousin" Eugene Walton's daily gospel programs, circa 1954. *Author's collection.*

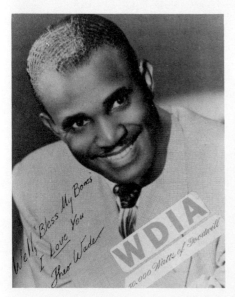

A singer and booking agent for the Spirit of Memphis, Theo Wade was best known as a WDIA disc jockey, circa 1952. *Author's collection.*

WDIA gospel disc jockey Ford Nelson, circa 1952, began his broadcasting career in the late 1940s. *Author's collection.*

In 1951 WDIA was featuring regular broadcasts by the Spirit of Memphis: "Little Ax" Broadnax, "Jet" Bledsoe, Robert Reed, James Darling, Earl Malone, Silas Steele. *Author's collection.*

The Spirit of Memphis reached the height of their popularity about 1953: (*top*) Fred Howard, "Jet" Bledsoe, Earl Malone; (*bottom*) Robert Reed, Silas Steele, "Little Ax" Broadnax, Theo Wade. *Author's collection.*

The Southern Wonders, circa 1953, did many remote broadcasts on WDIA sponsored by Pet Milk: (*standing*) L. T. Blair, Ernest McKinney, James Darling, Jack Franklin, R. L. Weaver, Artis Yancey; (*seated*) Ford Nelson. *Courtesy of Essie Mae Wade.*

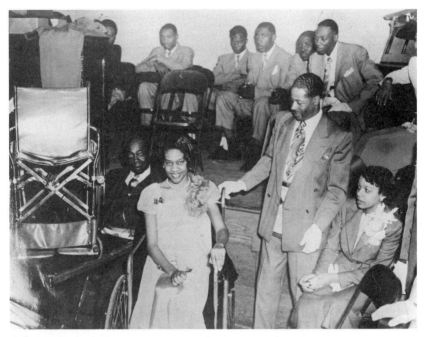

The Southern Wonders, seated on stage, performed at a benefit to purchase a new wheelchair for the young woman on the left. *Author's collection.*

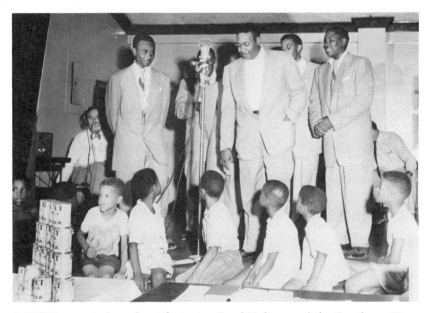

A WDIA remote broadcast featuring Ford Nelson and the Southern Wonders, from the Foote Homes in Memphis, circa 1952. *Author's collection.*

By 1953 the Southern Wonders recorded for Peacock Records: (*top*) Jack Franklin, Artis Yancey, R. L. Weaver; (*bottom*) Ernest McKinney, L. T. Blair, James Darling. *Author's collection.*

An unknown quartet performing on a WDIA remote broadcast, circa 1952. *Author's collection.*

The Spirit of Memphis posing with heavyweight boxing champion "Jersey Joe" Walcott, about 1953: Theo Wade, Fred Howard, Walcott, Robert Reed, Earl Malone, "Little Ax" Broadnax, "Jet" Bledsoe, Silas Steele. *Courtesy of Essie Mae Wade.*

The Dixie Nightingales, circa 1960, evolved from the Gospel Writer Junior Boys: (*top*) Ollie Hoskins, Willie Neal, Bill Davis; (*bottom*) Melvin Malone, Nelson Lesure, Rochester Neal. *Author's collection.*

The Sunset Travelers, about 1962, recorded for Peacock Records: (*top*) Clyde Beyers, Grover Blake, Robert Lewis; (*bottom*) Daniel Scott, Rev. Jeff Brown. *Courtesy of Doug Seroff.*

By 1956 the Spiritual Travelers had become a semiprofessional quartet: Levi Williams, Henry Bishop, L. D. Tennel, J. W. Williams, Sam Jones, Julius Readers. *Author's collection.*

SOUVENIR PROGRAM
1956
WDIA
Goodwill Revue
All-Star Charity Show

8:00 P.M. December 7th   Ellis Auditorium

KEEL AVE. SCHOOL   WDIA GOODWILL BUS
REVUE $ AT WORK
WDIA LEAGUE   R. HORNSBY CLINIC

Souvenir program, 1956 WDIA Goodwill Revue. *Author's collection.*

The WDIA Goodwill Fund

In 1949, Radio Station WDIA presented the first Goodwill Revue to provide aid to needy Negro children. This was the birth of the Goodwill Station policy to "help people to help themselves."

For the first four years, all profits were turned over to established Memphis charity funds. As the shows grew larger, the Revue moved into North Hall of Ellis Auditorium, and a larger charity project was sought. In 1954, the Fund was incorporated and plans made to enable WDIA to purchase, and operate special buses in order that Negro crippled children could get proper education. Now the Keel Avenue school is being operated by the Memphis Board of Education at the suggestion of WDIA.

In addition to this service for Negro Crippled Children, the year 1955 saw Goodwill at work in the field of juvenile sports. The Fund purchased 198 baseball uniforms and equipment for 14 teams—the WDIA Little League, first of its kind in the United States. This year, almost 400 youngsters played in the League.

This past summer, on July 3rd, the first annual "Starlight Revue" was presented at Martin Stadium before more than 11,000 people . . . who came and contributed to the Goodwill Fund.

These charity shows are produced and presented by the WDIA staff with the help of America's top recording stars who come to Memphis at their own expense. Absolutely NO ONE RECEIVES A CENT FOR HIS SERVICES. All money goes to the WDIA Goodwill Fund.

These projects are Goodwill at work . . . helping people in communities all over the Mid-South to help themselves to better education — better standards of living — better understanding—and better opportunity. Your ticket money is your contribution to all of these. This is Goodwill At Work.

Program

Part One: "A Pilgrimage To The Holy Land"

Ford Nelson	Theo Wade
Cornell Wells	Ernest Brazzle

Aunt Carrie

The Brewsteraires	Dixie Nightengales
Unison Voices	Reed Singers
Sons Of Jehovah	Friendly Echoes

THE SPIRIT OF MEMPHIS
REV. CLEOPHUS ROBINSON
MADAME ROBINSON
THE HAPPYLAND BLIND BOYS

****

Part Two: Early American Rock'n Roll
Blues and Pop Stars

WDIA Goodwill Revue All-Star Band

RAY CHARLES..Atlantic Records
THE MAGNIFICENTS..Vee-Jay Records
B. B. KING...WDIA-RPM
THE MOONGLOWS..Chess Records

THE CAST

Great Googa Mooga (Medicine Man)	Nat Williams
Sweet Mama	Willa Monroe
Big Chief Moohah	Moohah
Chief Rockin' Horse	Rufus Thomas
Princess Premium Stuff	Martha Jean
Crazy Man Crazy	Honeyboy
Bad Stuff	Cathryn Johnson
Braves and Squaws	Teen Town Singers

Costumes: Mattie Lee Russell, Martha Armstrong, Betty Mattis, Yvonne Brown.

THE STORY: Big Chief Moohah is an old-fashioned Indian who does not approve of rock'n roll. This new musical influence has been brought into Choctaw tribe by Chief Rockin' Horse who has run off and married Princess Premium Stuff, daughter of Big Chief. For that, Rockin' Horse and all braves have been banished from tribe.

WDIA Goodwill family portrait. *Author's collection.*

The WDIA Goodwill Story

From 1070 on your radio dial, you hear the friendly voice of RADIO
STATION WDIA in Memphis, broadcasting with <u>50,000 watts</u> of power--
<u>the most powerful</u> radio station possible -- on the air from 4:00 A.M.
to 12 midnight.

You hear the wonderful programs and sparkling stars that have made
WDIA the favorite station of more than half a million Negroes in and
around Memphis for more than six years!

WDIA, The Goodwill Station, is the FIRST -- and the ONLY 50,000-watt
station programmed exclusively for Negroes, -- truly one of America's
GREAT radio stations!

But WDIA has many other "firsts" to its credit, too. It pioneered in
Negro programming and was the first station to devote all of its time
to serving Negroes. WDIA had the first all-Negro staff of broadcast
stars, "Brown America Speaks" (the first all-Negro forum for the free
and open discussion of Negro problems), and the first Negro woman
broadcaster in America. WDIA is first in public service promotion
for Negroes, and has received outstanding recognition and awards.

WDIA has the largest Negro audience in America; a listening audience
wanting the best entertainment and programs in the nation. Known as
"The Starmaker Station" for development of Negro talent, WDIA has
discovered such recording stars as B. B. King, Johnny ACE, Rosco
Gordon, Earl Forest and Bobby Bland. WDIA was directly responsible
for the development of gospel groups such as Teen Town Singers, The
Spirit of Memphis Quartet, The Southern Wonders, The Songbirds of
The South, -- all presently heard on WDIA. Every week, you hear the
Southern Jubilee Singers, The Brewsteraires, Brother Cleophas
Robinson, The Friendly Echoes, The Jones Boys, The Gospel Writer
Jr. Boys, and many other outstanding singers.

WDIA has been called "the sensation of the nation" by many, but WDIA
calls itself YOUR GOODWILL STATION, and by that name it is known
by the 3,800,000 people in its tremendous listening area.

First in Negro programming with 50,000 watts, -- first in the hearts
of its listeners, WDIA is YOUR station. DAYTIME and NIGHTTIME,
TOO -- 1070 on your radio.

1070

| 55 | 60 | 70 | 90 ▼ | 110 | 130 | 150 |

Set Your Radio Dial

The Spirit of Memphis's popularity continued well into the late 1950s:
(*top*) Robert Reed, Fred Howard, "Jet" Bledsoe, Earl Malone; (*bottom*)
O. V. Wright, Berry Brown. *Author's collection.*

TNT Braggs, Don Robey, and Bobby "Blue" Bland (*left to right*), circa
1955. *Courtesy of Michael Ochs Archives/Venice, California.*

CHAPTER

4

"A Family of Singers"

Over the years the black gospel quartet singers in Memphis have evolved into a highly complex, extended family by virtue of birth, marriage, geographic proximity, religious affiliation, and shared social values and status. These singers, the organizers of gospel "quartet unions," and the quartet trainers are among the core members of the unique musical community to be explored in this chapter.

To date, few American studies utilizing the concept of a musical community have been published.[1] Such a community can be described as a loose-knit, often eclectic group of people coalescing around a shared, specific musical interest. We have, for example, Alan Merriam and Raymond Mack's analysis of "the set of people who share an interest in jazz, and who share it at a level of intensity such that they participate to some extent in the occupation role and ideology of the professional jazz musician. They learn and accept at least some of the norms which are particular to the jazz musician: norms regarding proper and improper language, good and bad music, stylish and unstylish clothing, acceptable and unacceptable audience behavior and so forth."[2] Bill Ferris has studied, among other groups, the musical community of blues singers that existed in Leland, Mississippi, during the 1960s. He remarks that "the blues community grew up like a family with a kinship of love for music and good times together."[3] These comments reflect some of my own thoughts regarding the Memphis gospel quartet community, which encompasses not only the singers themselves but disc jockeys, preachers, record company officials, and fans, as well as relatives of the singers. Indeed, anyone with more than a casual connection with Memphis gospel quartets is part of this unique musical community.

Quartet and other gospel singers often speak to one another using the ritualistic church greetings "brother" and "sister." Doug Seroff, who has also written about black gospel quartets in Memphis, observed that "it would not be misleading to describe Memphis' gospel singing community as a 'family.' The local gospel scene was rather insular and surprisingly homogeneous."[4] His suggestion that gospel singers form a "family" is quite often literally true: many of the local quartet singers have married others who have also been in singing groups; in fact, of the fifty singers interviewed for this book, 60 percent had married within the Memphis quartet community. Cleo and Louis Satterfield are a typical quartet couple. They first met in 1941 at a gospel quartet program—Louis was a member of the True Friends Gospel Singers and Cleo sang with the Union Soft Singers. Within two years they had wed. Elijah Jones and his first wife, Jimmie Martin, became acquainted in the late 1930s when he led the Gospel Writers and she performed with the Gospel Writer Junior Girls. Some of the most important and influential singers in Memphis—Jethroe and Shirley Bledsoe, James and Elizabeth Darling, Floyd and Florence Wiley—also were involved with gospel quartets both before and after their marriages.

Kinship patterns within the quartet community are not limited only to married couples, however, for many siblings have been involved with singing. Willie and Rochester Neal began their careers in the late 1940s as members of the Gospel Writer Junior Boys under the direction of their stepfather, Elijah Jones. They continued with this group throughout the 1950s and 1960s, weathering many personnel changes and a switch in name to the Dixie Nightingales. When the group turned to popular music in the middle 1960s, both Neal brothers left to join the Pattersonaires. Clara and Essie Anderson were sisters who began singing together with the Busyline Soft Singers during the mid-1930s and sang with a neighborhood quartet until Essie's death in 1938. Clara remained in singing and went on to form the Golden Stars and then the

Harps of Melody. Doris Jean Gary was a vital member of the Songbirds of the South between 1949 and 1956, while her brother Willie sang first with the Rust College Quartet and then helped to found the Pattersonaires in 1953.

Although familial involvement in black gospel music is not limited to quartets or to Memphis—for example, the Staple Singers from Mississippi and Alabama's Ravizee Singers, two long-respected black American gospel groups, have been composed entirely or almost entirely of members from the same family—it is nonetheless striking how pervasive kinship systems are within the Memphis musical community. Despite the size of the city, its position as a transportation hub, and its importance as a destination for migrants in the Mid-South, the quartet community in Memphis has remained largely free of outside influence.

The Memphis quartet community has long extended well beyond kinship systems into more practical concerns of cooperation, one of the most visible and interesting being the formation of "unions" to cultivate quartet singing within the city. While organizations like the National Convention of Gospel Choirs and Choruses, Inc., which Thomas A. Dorsey founded in Chicago in 1932, existed to promote large ensembles, smaller groups also formed to encourage unity among quartets. For example, in Chicago, just before the Great Depression, Norman McQueen began a quartet union that was probably America's first such organization.

The first quartet organization in Memphis was the City Quartette Union, founded by "Doctor" Frost in 1939. Although not a singer himself, Frost took a lively interest in harmony singing. He helped to organize and promote weekly programs within the city and often served as master of ceremonies. The City Quartette Union lost his valuable services in 1943 when Frost migrated to Detroit for a more lucrative daytime job. Another charter member of the organization, James Darling, assumed Frost's responsibilities for about four years. Then Huddie Moore replaced Darling, holding the presidency of the City Quartette Union until its dissolution in about 1953. Moore explains the ideology and organization of the union: The idea was "to get a lot of singers together and cooperate, and have more people participate on your programs. When you had the City Quartette Union and the quartets, you had your program. All you had to get [was] the church and render your program. We'd have the City Quartette Union [chorus] open the program and let the quartets come on later."[5]

Although it was the first organization of its kind in Memphis, the City Quartette Union was not the only group to serve as the community's rallying point and clearinghouse for quartet singing. Most of the older singers I interviewed mentioned two similar groups—the South Memphis Singing Union and the North Memphis Singing Union—which existed briefly during the mid-1940s but proved to be so ephemeral that nothing more can be learned about them. Just after the end of World War II, however, another more substantial, influential cooperative, the United Singing Union, was formed. Several singers suggested that this organization sprang up in the wake of the South Memphis Singing Union. Regardless of its origins, the United Singing Union was a very significant force in organizing the Memphis community-based quartets throughout the late 1940s and 1950s.

The guiding strength behind the United Singing Union, from its inception until the early 1980s, was Lillian Wafford. Although greatly burdened by her husband's severe stroke in 1978, Mrs. Wafford worked tirelessly to keep the union together and functioning smoothly. During her tenure she served as the union's president and its spiritual leader. Mrs. Wafford nursed her husband until his death in March 1982, and within ten days she herself was dead. With its principal leadership gone, Memphis's last gospel quartet cooperative disbanded.

The principal purposes of these unions were to encourage solidarity among members, promote quartet singing, and assist members in booking their programs. While their goals were concrete, the organizations themselves were not always so stable. According to Mary Davis, cofounder in 1944 of the Majestic Soft Singers, the ranks of the United Singing Union were always in flux: "The original group was the Majestic Soft Singers plus the Spiritual Pilgrims. Then came the Wells Spirituals . . . then the Morris Special Singers . . . [and] four or five years later, the Brewsteraires. Then we had the Walker Specials to join in. In other words, we had several groups to going in, but several of them didn't stay too long."[6] These continual changes created a fluid organization whose precise ranks are impossible to establish. Mrs. Wafford left no formal, written records, though it appears that only the Wells Spirituals, the Majestic Soft Singers, and the Spiritual Pilgrims remained union members for an extended period.

It is apparent that once the United Singing Union established its reputation as a clearinghouse for booking quartets in the late 1940s, it served an important and useful purpose in Memphis. Mrs. Wafford, who oversaw the union's finances, had a formula for splitting fees between the host group and the quartet. Basically, programs held in Memphis paid 50 percent of the money to the quartet and 50 percent to the host church, while programs held outside of Memphis paid 60 percent to the quartet, with the host church receiving 40 percent; the difference reflected the travel expenses involved. Out of the revenues from programs booked by the United Singing Union, each quartet contributed some money to the union for organizational expenses. Mrs. Wafford herself accepted no salary; she considered her work as a contribution to the union as well as a means of assisting others in spreading this musical ministry.

The spirit of cooperation and mutual assistance that characterized the City Quartette Union and the United Singing Union was emblematic of a more general sense of a synergetic partnership that permeated the black American gospel quartet community in Memphis. Although singing was the focal point for their energies, group members were also deeply involved in service to the community at large. Both major quartet unions fit into a larger mosaic of the city's black religious community that served as the center of social and community work long before President Johnson's cry for the Great Society brought us a codified welfare system and Aid to Dependent Children. In this respect the unions deserve to be viewed in the same light as African Method Episcopal (A.M.E.) women's auxiliary groups or local civic and fraternal organizations, which also served as self-help groups in the black community. The church and its many allied support services have been the backbone of black social and religious life for many decades, extending their community work in Memphis far beyond a strictly sacred context.

The comments of Cleo Satterfield illustrate the important role of gospel quartet unions in the social and cultural fabric of black life:

Frost [of the City Quartette Union] was the type of person who could keep a program so alive that everybody wanted to hear him talk after the singing. He was nice about helping someone if he knew they were sick or somebody in the group or in the church was sick. It somebody tell him about it, he would raise an offering for them. If they knew that something was wrong with someone they knew, they would always reach out and give a helping hand. We never had that much, but what we had, we'd give it freely. If you were in the city, if you got to a program, you always help somebody.[7]

Huddie Moore recalls that the City Quartette Union "would do a program for somebody who had gotten burned out or something like that. We would put on programs to raise money to help that family or different things like that. Somebody was always in necessity."[8] He also observed that a share of the money from each program the union sponsored went into a special fund, and at Christmas union members would deliver baskets of food to needy families.

The aid provided by these gospel groups included spiritual sustenance as well, particularly in the form of free programs held at rest homes and senior citizens' centers. Some quartets even performed in local prisons and jails, the idea being simply to spread the ministry of God in song. Etherlene Beans explains how she and her group, the Willing Four Softline Singers, worked:

They contacted us because they find that we were just a group that liked to sing. We didn't sing for finances . . . [but because] we like to sing and we always want to share what we had with other people. We was really a spiritual group. We like to sing and get happy and let other people get happy. We just would go where we thought that the spirit was needed. We would go to the workhouse and sing . . . also sing for sick people, cripple children's hospitals, and to help churches.

I like to sing quartet singing because I'm a Christian person and I believe in feeling spiritually. I sing until I feel good . . . and feel like I've helped somebody. I want to try and save a soul, see, through my singing.[9]

By the late 1940s a nationwide group, the National Quartet Convention, was founded by the Famous Blue Jay Singers and the Soul Stirrers for the purpose of "professionalizing" gospel quartets. Headquartered in Chicago, chapters were quickly established throughout the country. In 1949 a Memphis chapter was formed; its first president was Floyd Wiley. The impact of this nationwide group on Memphis quartets was significant, though it had a different premise from that of the local singing organizations. While the City Quartette Union and the United Singing Union were primarily interested in supporting local groups and providing social assistance, the National Quartet Convention stressed a professional stance toward quartet singing. The convention's annual meeting featured workshops and sessions devoted to helping groups develop or improve their organizational and business skills. A member of the National Quartet Convention since the early 1950s, Flozell Leland, explains: "We have workshops that train you how to do a whole lot of things; how to meet people, how to address an audience, how to perform, how to dress, and, really, how to sing; how to do a lot of [related] things: carry meetings, make motions and what not. A lot of people don't even know how to be a secretary or write a 'minute.' That's very important."[10]

The efforts of the National Quartet Convention to promote professionalism among quartet singers were not lost on Memphis, though it was a lesson that many local groups had already learned. Like the whole community of singers, the quartets themselves generally follow formal rules of protocol and procedure similar to those found in social and civic clubs. Quartets contain anywhere from four to eight members who delegate among themselves the duties and responsibilities necessary to operate. Memphis quartets tend to divide the responsibilities among four parties: manager, secretary, treasurer, and president. The manager is in charge of choosing uniforms, sound equipment, and any other similar items required by the group. The manager also helps with the details of transportation to and from the program, decides if infractions, such as chewing gum in church or missing a rehearsal, deserve fines, and serves as one of the liaisons between the group and anyone wishing to book programs.

The primary role of the quartet president is to oversee meetings and rehearsals. This includes reading minutes from the previous meeting, calling for new business, reading the roll call, and clarifying any questions or problems that arise. The president is also the quartet's public spokesperson. If the president is ill, then the manager fills in. The secretary records each meeting's minutes, including the time and location, which members are absent, and what fines are levied. Another duty is to keep track of the bylaws, to which new rules can be added or old rules deleted, according to a vote of the membership. The quartet treasurer accounts for all funds and keeps track of all travel expenses, the cost of uniforms, fines, dues, income from programs, and so forth. He or she is also charged with collecting money and dispersing funds.

To complement this formal hierarchy, local quartets have a set of rules (either written or tacitly understood) by which they govern themselves. Some rules pertain strictly to the procedural matters needed to run meetings, while others help to maintain order and stability within the group. These bylaws or club rules are important tools in the struggle to keep singers from "backsliding" and for promoting group solidarity. While almost every Memphis quartet has a system of laws, some groups operate under casual, somewhat loose regulations. Others like the Harps of Melody and the Gospel Writers, have strict codes.

BYLAWS
For the Harps of Melody—Adopted Sept. 13, 1950.
I. Every member of the Harps of Melody must be a member of some church and in good standing with her church.
II. Every member of the Harps of Melody must show a spirit of unity and fellowship which means love and care towards each other and all on one accord.
III. Rehearsal time shall be from 8:00 to 10:45 pm. Every member is responsible for making sure that all meetings and rehearsals are strictly private as possible when meeting in the home, unless there is a prospective member involved.
IV. Each member of the Harps of Melody must be on time as much as possible for rehearsals and programs.
V. Any member interrupting while another member is talking in meetings or rehearsals shall be supervised.
VI. Every member of the Harps of Melody is asked not to smoke in public or on church property or any public place, or chew gum on program.
VII. Realizing that the public has its eye on the Harps of Melody every member must respect and obey officers on programs and in public places.
VIII. Any member discussing any business or secrets of the Harps of Melody with any other than the members of the group shall be suspended.

IX. Any member that creates a disturbance while on program or in rehearsal or humiliate the Harps of Melody in any way shall be dealt with as the group sees fit.

X. Every member must be clean and neat in appearance on all programs, and uniform must be becoming.

XI. Any member of the Harps of Melody using profanity in the meetings, programs, rehearsals or any public place shall be suspended.

XII. Whenever the Harps of Melody appear on program each member must always perform to the best of her skill and ability. We must always pray and ask the Spirit of God to dwell with us at all times.

XIII. Any member who misses 3 meetings and come in on the 4th meeting with a good reason will be heard by the group and do as the group see fit.

By-Laws for the Gospel Writers

I. Business Meeting and Rehearsal every Saturday at 5:00 PM.
   A. Order of the Meeting:
      1. Devotion by the Chaplain.
      2. Business meeting carried out by the President.
      3. Rehearsal under the supervision of the manager.

II. All members are under the direction of the manager at all times except during the business meeting.

III. Each member is required to pay weekly dues.

IV. Each member is required to meet on time at all of the group's engagements or meetings.

V. All members are to be uniformed.

VI. Each member is required to carry himself in such a manner, so as not to downgrade or disgrace this group in any way.

VII. Each member is required to fully support this group both spiritually and financially to the best of his ability.

These bylaws cover a multitude of problems and sins and allow the group to exert some leverage over members who break the rules. Although punishment for infractions is not explicitly covered, monetary fines determined by the president are most often levied. Serious offenses generally mean a higher fine, and if the affront is grievous enough, then a member can be suspended or dropped from the quartet. Along with internal order, quartets are also concerned with their public image, as is underscored by their rules related to public decorum and dress. The quartet singers have carefully shaped and cultivated a finely tuned image, that of respectful and forthright Christians who dress well, in the height of fashion.

It is difficult to ascertain precisely how the rules and club system evolved. The first of Memphis's black quartets to record, the I.C. Glee Club, consciously referred to itself as a "club." Many of the quartet veterans whose careers date back to the 1920s and 1930s—Elijah Ruffin, Clara Anderson, Luther McGill, and James Harvey—also frequently refer to older groups as clubs. In their heyday many quartets were closely or directly associated with neighborhood churches, local companies, or neighborhood groups—for example, the Jolly Sunshine Boosters Club Quartet, which was part of a well-known south Memphis civic club in the late 1940s. Such connections help to account for the quartets' formal rules, their internal structures, and their strict hierarchies.

Another aspect of the close-knit nature of this musical community is the way in which quartets are trained. Quartet training is very demanding, requiring extremely specialized skills. The process is critical because it involves the transmission of musical repertoire and style. By preserving certain musical traits, quartet trainers also provide a crucial link between one generation of musicians and another, as well as links between groups. At first glance the role of gospel quartet trainers appears quite simple—they teach songs. But their functions are actually far more detailed and complex. Trainers have long been regarded as specialists by quartet singers, who initially called upon them for several reasons. One was to help groups orient new members. Etherlene Beans of the Willing Four Softline Singers says that Elijah Jones was often asked to attend their rehearsals when new members were being trained. Groups also requested that trainers aid them in learning new songs or arrangements; thus the trainer assisted with the intricacies of vocal timbre, rhythm, and harmony—three of the key ingredients in gospel quartet singing. If a trainer developed a new arrangement that proved popular, other local groups often asked him to provide them with the same or similar arrangement.

Trainers have sometimes been asked to locate new singers for groups, though most groups recruit members themselves. For many years Elijah Jones served as the unofficial coordinator for quartets that needed new singers, and when Huddie Moore was forming the Memphis Spiritual Four in the middle 1930s, Jones did not wait to be asked but stepped forward and volunteered his services. Clara Anderson recalls that Jones's mentor, Gus Miller, offered to help the Busyline Soft Singers. Similar observations regarding the eagerness of quartet trainers to help groups have been made by many other Memphis singers, which suggests that the trainers saw themselves as providing a unique and invaluable service to the community as well as propagating the music they loved.

Although they were often very busy helping quartets and spent innumerable hours in this service, trainers were not motivated by the prospect of financial rewards. All of the Memphis trainers have been singers, though none of them forged a full-time living from gospel music. Gus Miller, for example, survived with the help of his family and a veteran's pension he received as the result of a severe wound sustained in World War I. Elijah Jones spent his entire life as a blue-collar worker. Some trainers may have been offered money for their services, but this was strictly a free-will offering. Etherlene Beans notes that Elijah Jones "never did get money from us. Now, in late days, we used to give him a little money, a little transportation money on his gas, but he never made money off us. He just likes singing . . . and he was always willing to assist us in singing." [11]

This observation provides the key to the motivation of quartet trainers. While some people were able organizers or willing to publicize events, these talented men loved harmony singing and their help was a gift to their fellow singers. George Rooks, who knew and sang with Elijah Jones off and on for nearly forty years, recalls that Jones stood at the nexus of the quartet community. Most weekends found him singing or attending a quartet program or a rehearsal. Trainers of Miller's and Jones's stature were also frequently asked to judge "quartet contests" (a performance event to be discussed shortly).

Being recognized by one's peers as a trainer denotes a special status within this musical community. Gospel quartet trainers are blessed with unusually perceptive ears and minds and the ability to communicate their knowledge. When groups regularly come to certain individuals asking for assistance, this acknowledges the community's respect for their talents. It is evident that Memphis trainers have enjoyed intuitive skills honed through practice and application rather than through formal education. Elijah Ruffin, who has worked with about a dozen local groups, considers his training ability a natural gift, albeit one shaped by nearly five decades of experience. Most quartet singers are self-taught or have learned through an apprenticeship system that has nothing to do with formally graded musical education. Some singers may aspire to become trainers, but first they must be accepted by their peers.

As I have already intimated, males have dominated quartet training in Memphis. Indeed, the singers I interviewed did not mention women in their discussions of training specialists, except for women such as Clara Anderson, who worked with the Harps of Melody and Golden Stars, who did train their own groups. One result of this male-dominated training system is that Memphis's female quartets almost always refer to their voices as bass, baritone, alto, and lead. It is at first startling to hear women's parts called baritone or bass, but this terminology is so commonplace in Memphis that it quickly loses its novelty. The practice is perhaps best explained by the fact that quartet trainers "give" people their voices; that is, they often assign each person to a vocal range. Thus the trainers designate the lowest female voice, like the lowest male voice, as bass.

The fundamental process of training quartets is itself relatively easy to describe—the trainer simply sings each part to all of the singers in turn and then the singers blend the parts in four-part harmony. Long-time Memphis trainer Jack Miller articulates the process: "The first thing is the voice. Check the voices out; see if the voice is fitted for a tenor, baritone, lead or bass. Then you go from there. You have to sing the four voices to get the pitch of the song, to teach it. Then you work on the time of the songs, how long you should go with it. Some people are quick to catch on, some are not. If they got the talent to catch on and the voice, then you train them in a couple months."[12] While the procedure sounds simple, it demands an unusual knowledge and skill. First, the trainer must be able to sing each of the four voices; in fact, trainers have often filled the role of "utility singers" in their own quartets. Second, the trainer intuitively conceives harmonies, rhythms, and tempos, a process that is refined and adjusted as the parts are taught to the group. Finally, the lack of a notation system means that the trainers work entirely through oral means, relying heavily upon tonal memory and sheer repetition. Training a quartet absolutely requires an immense amount of skill as well as a willingness to invest a great deal of time, concentration, and energy.

The most renowned and influential trainer in Memphis, Elijah Jones, worked with countless groups during his career. Etherlene Beans describes how Jones helped the Willing Four Softline Singers:

> He would train you how to control your voice, how to keep your voice with the next singer, not to get too loud for the next singer, not to get too loud for your music [instruments], not to get your music too loud for you. I have a loud voice and he always taught me to tone my voice down so that I wouldn't drown the other singers out. He always teach us to say our words distinctly, not to drag through them. He always teach you to sing words distinctly, and you cannot sing a song unless you know it. He helped us a whole lot. It was just remarkable what he could do with singers.[13]

Trainers also are noted for their suggestions regarding vocal and tonal qualities or techniques. For instance, a trainer might advise that the featured singer affect a more raspy tonal color or sing his or her part falsetto; a trainer could make the arrangement of a song distinctive by altering the tempo during the chorus or by having the background sung more staccato.

Groups would call upon the services of trainers for extended periods of time, as Leon Moody of the Jolly Sunshine Boosters Club Quartet recalls:

> For years and years we would go to Gus [Miller] and he would okay each of the songs that we'd rehearse. You can go so far with a group, after you stay together long enough, you can mighty near tell yourself when you are getting off at all. We got to the point where . . . if one fellow missed a note or key or something, it might take us 30 or 40 minutes or maybe an hour. But we would change it or correct it. After so long we would go back to Gus, maybe once or twice a month and he would . . . check us.[14]

The groups themselves utilized such basic ideas in their ongoing struggle to achieve "their own sound." The spark of creativity frequently began with the trainers, but suggestions from within the group often carried it forward. Radical changes in the styles of Memphis quartet singing, particularly prior to World War II, came slowly. When quartets began functioning in the realm of popular culture during the 1940s and 1950s, however, the local appearances of touring groups, records, and radio created an atmosphere for more rapid innovation.

Despite this ongoing emphasis on innovation among certain Memphis quartets, trainers never lost their prestige or influence within the local quartet community. Elijah Jones remained in demand as a trainer until his death in January 1980. Long after the "boom years" of quartet singing, many Memphis quartets still wished to learn the art of harmony singing from this acknowledged master. The other master trainer was Gus Miller, who spent his adult life confined to a wheelchair. His participation in World War I suggests a birthdate circa 1890 and possibly accounts for his disability. Elijah Jones recalled that Miller sang with and had trained the Harmony Four when they first met in the late 1920s. Gus Miller's half-brother, Frank (a former quartet singer now living in St. Louis), reports that during the 1920s and 1930s Gus shuttled back and forth between Memphis and St. Louis, where he had a married daughter. Little more is known of Miller's personal life except that he apparently died in Memphis around 1960.

We do know quite a lot about Miller's influential work with several local groups during the 1930s. Because of his infirmity, he was unable to sing for extended periods, though he was a member of at least one group, the legendary Middle Baptist Quartet, after the Harmony Four split up in the early 1930s. James Harvey recollects Miller's skill as a trainer: "Gus was almost as good as Elijah Jones. I think if Gus would have kept it up, he would have been as good as Elijah. He was dedicated to it. There is something about group work that you've got to hear a song . . . you just hear the tune and put it together. He was just that type person; he could do that. It seem like a talent he have [and] could share with somebody else."[15] Elijah Ruffin, Clara Anderson, and others active during the depression years also recall Gus Miller with great respect. They speak of a period when Miller, rather than Jones, was the busiest trainer in Memphis.

Due to increasingly ill health, Miller's work as a trainer greatly diminished during the years following World War II, and he was quickly replaced by his talented apprentice, Elijah Jones. Born in Millington, Tennessee, in 1906, Jones moved to Memphis with his family in 1924. The sound of harmony singing fascinated him and he soon became immersed in the quartet community. By 1928 he was working as a laborer and singing: "When we were around home, we were always singing around the house. I began to say

'I'm going to get to singing.' I picked up one or two fellows and we sat around and singed. I didn't know nothing about singing then, just picked it up. After I sang it, it comed to me more. So I got to where I could separate voices. Once I could separate voices, it give me a gift and then I could train voices. I got where I could sing all voices myself." [16]

Although considered a good singer, Elijah Jones's most important contribution to Memphis harmony singing was undoubtedly his role as a trainer. He started his own group, the Gospel Writers, in the late 1930s but was soon training another group for young women, the Gospel Writer Junior Girls. This group eventually became the Songbirds of the South, one of the most respected female groups in Memphis quartet history. A similar story can be told of the Gospel Writer Junior Boys, which changed its name to the Dixie Nightingales in the early 1950s and went on to enjoy an impressive career. It is difficult even to estimate how many groups Jones worked with during the peak of his career, but it must have been a score or more.

In the middle 1950s, for reasons unknown, Jones disbanded the Gospel Writers and absented himself from quartet singing for nearly twenty years. He still occasionally helped train groups but not nearly as readily as he once did. Equally enigmatic was his 1976 reemergence, which marked a revival of the Gospel Writers and his return to active quartet training. Perhaps this flurry of activity was a presentiment of his fatal heart attack in 1980. Whatever the reasons, his work between 1976 and 1980 helped to reactivate the groups stressing older, more conservative singing and performance styles.

Afro-American gospel quartets have always emphasized performance and communication with their audience. Hence, performance events provide a vital key to understanding this music and its importance to members of the black community in Memphis. Quartet programs are the most common medium for the public to hear and see these singers. Nearly every Sunday and on many Saturdays since the 1920s, Memphis gospel quartets have appeared in churches and auditoriums throughout the city. Although all quartets have some direct affiliation with churches, either as church-related groups or simply as members of a church, they have not always appeared as part of the worship service itself. In fact, congregational singing or choirs most often present the musical offering during regularly scheduled services.

Quartets in Memphis usually perform on special musical programs held during the afternoons or evenings, which often feature more than one ensemble. In a very real sense quartet programs constitute an extension of the Sunday morning worship service, the difference being the programs' emphasis on music as the instrument by which to worship God. Local quartet programs typically last between one and three hours. They are promoted within the black church community by way of placards, posters, notices in the church bulletins and newspapers, announcements from the pulpit, over the radio, and during other programs, and by word-of-mouth. If more than one group is involved, the guests sing first while the host quartet remains to finish the program and to assist in closing the church.

The other type of quartet program in Memphis involves out-of-town groups brought in especially to perform. Both programs are similar in the way they are promoted and the places in which they are held. There are, however, some very critical contextual differences. Although both local and out-of-town programs feature quartet singing, they are not truly analogous. The major programs held at the City Auditorium, the Mason's Temple, and the large churches in Memphis have been religious music events *and* popular entertainment. Especially during the fifteen years following the end of World War II, the popular professional quartets were prominent members of the greater black community and some were as well known as their secular counterparts. Attendance at programs and the frequency with which their records or live performances were heard over the radio confirmed certain groups' popularity. Personal appearances in Memphis by these quartets provided an occasion for religious worship in song and the opportunity to see "stars" perform.

This performance context is very different from a program by local groups like the Royal Harmony Four, the Keystone Masters of Harmony, or any one of a number of other Memphis quartets active during the postwar years. While the basic premise of praising the Lord in song is identical, the difference is more than simply the facile distinction between a local and a professional quartet. One group sings for a community of relatives, peers, and neighbors in a local church, while the other gospel quartet works in a larger, more spacious setting for an audience with whom they have had little, if any, direct personal contact.

Members of Memphis's quartet community are aware of this distinction. Because money and prestige are involved, a program headlined by a non-Memphis quartet such as the Five Blind Boys of Mississippi or the Dixie Hummingbirds is perceived as a special event. Singers from these quartets are considered specialists because they make at least part of their livelihood from music. Memphian Willie Neal speaks of the need to balance spiritual and material desires:

> That's what gospel quartet is all about—being a Christian. It don't mean perfect. . . . We [the Dixie Nightingales] had sung with the top groups of the decade—the Dixie Hummingbirds, the Mighty Clouds of Joy, the Five Blind Boys, the Spirit of Memphis, all those groups. Some of these groups have really made it big, but we are still the more humble gospel.
>
> It is my personal belief that salvation is free. I was singing gospel songs and I was singing from the heart; but in the back of my mind, I was also looking for that dollar. That doesn't mean that you can't do it [make money], but it's what's in your heart and that has to do with the spirit. The spirit is not the dollar.[17]

In fact, local quartet unions and promoters of major programs did use the money that they had raised from concerts in different ways—aptly illustrating Neal's point. A certain portion of this money always went back into the community, but the amounts differed greatly. The City Quartette Union, for instance, assisted people within Memphis neighborhoods and gave food to the needy at Christmas. The United Singing Union fulfilled much the same function during the 1950s. By contrast, the money raised by ticket sales for programs involving professional groups primarily went to cover a variety of expenses including hall rental, advertising, the promoters' percentage, and the groups' fee. A local church or group often cosponsored these programs, taking responsibility for some of the promotions and part of the other financial obligations in return for a percentage of the profits.

Despite these subtle though notable differences between the two types of programs, both performance events have many similarities. Specifically, they are cultural ceremonies by quartet singers with religious worship as the primary goal. These performances have always been regularly scheduled public events featuring highly trained and well-regarded singers. As cultural events, quartet programs are complex and are structured according to a clearly established format with three essential "players": the emcee (or master of ceremonies), the quartets, and the audience. The program itself opens with a well-known song led by the emcee, a minister, or a quartet member and performed by everyone in the audience. This helps to establish a feeling of fellowship among the participants. A prayer offered by one of the ministers then follows the opening song.

The role of an emcee is to assure that the quartets appear in the correct order, to keep the program moving on time, and to make proper introductions. The emcee also fills in the time between groups, while equipment is being changed and the quartets are getting set up, with announcements of future programs, light-hearted jokes, and brief testimonials (sometimes called "recognitions") for people attending the program. This person is clearly a specialist, often someone known within the community who has fulfilled this role before. Emcees are generally male and are often disc jockeys or in some way affiliated with the mass media. Occasionally an individual from outside this fraternity, such as "Doctor" Frost with the City Quartette Union, takes this role, but more often it is someone like Theo "Bless My Bones" Wade from WDIA or "Cousin" Eugene (Walton) of KWEM. For strictly local programs one of the group members or a clergyman frequently serves as the master of ceremonies.

Quartet programs generally start slowly and build in intensity. Much of the success of this type of cultural performance depends upon the interaction between the quartet and the audience. By the 1950s almost all Memphis quartets, and certainly each of the out-of-town groups, stressed stage presence with well-choreographed and well-planned performances. Quartet singing, particularly after the advent of touring professionals, also has been an emotional experience. The singers gesture to the audience and speak with them either directly or through sermonettes pioneered in the late 1940s by Silas Steele, and the audience responds in kind. This interaction is vividly recalled by Tommie Todd, who sang with the Gospel Writers following World War II:

> When we would go and render our programs, a lot of times we'd get converts. A lot of times people would join church on our singing. That's the reason I liked it, because there was something in it I could feel, that other people could feel. That's the reason it had such a pull. So many people would come to hear us because we would give them something that was a help to them. We would have our prayer service just like revival, then we'd go from there. When we got into our singing, people would be shouting. One time they got shouting so bad until a lady got hold to the wrong end of my tie and pulled . . . choked me! When we got singing like that they'd be shouting and throwing pocketbooks and things like that.[18]

Long before black popular singers such as Little Richard, Wilson Pickett, and James Brown gained the limelight, professional quartet singers like Silas Steele and "Jet" Bledsoe of the Spirit of Memphis were highly respected for their ability to "work" an audience. Their performances combined stage presence, singing, and visual techniques calculated to motivate and engage the crowd. Visual techniques included carefully rehearsed movements on stage, crawling along the floor, and walking on the benches among the audience, which was a distant cry from the descriptions of more sedate programs held during the 1920s and 1930s and bears the distinctive marks of the showmanship and bravado of professional quartet singers.

The frantic nature of post–World War II and professional quartets bothered older quartet singers like Leon Moody, who possessed a different sense of what quartet singing should be:

> These other guys went to using a guitar, maybe take a verse or two and then they would run the chorus 15 or 20 times. We sung a song, it lasted 3 or 4 minutes. Every song we sung, we tried to tell a message. We figured that in every song we sung, if we couldn't give them something to think about, that song wasn't worth singing.
>
> Some people just get up and go for a lot of Hallelujah. Most generally [those people] . . . go for guitars and a whole lot of noise. They do a lot of performing, a lot of show. I think if it is supposed to be a religious program it should be a service.[19]

It would be facile to simply dismiss certain stage techniques as stylized antics. Professionalism undeniably has changed the character of black gospel quartet performances, but the singers still draw inspiration from older role models. It is clear that some of these characteristics—dramatic body gestures, emotional vocal styles, and flamboyant behavior—can also be partially attributed to the Pentecostal movement and to African ritual. These aspects of black religious culture provide a model of emotional worship that has been present in Afro-American culture for many decades— the ring shout, the chanted sermon, and holy dancing.[20]

Along with singing and visual effects, quartet performances have also utilized other related verbal techniques. Perhaps the most affecting is the stage patter or speech that quartet singers use in addressing the audience. This mode of communicating is different from the everyday speech heard on the streets and contains many ornate phrases and biblical references; it is often formulaic as well. Although no one explicitly teaches quartet singers this way of speaking, the communicative mode, though not so long and cohesive, is reminiscent of the St. Vincent "sweet talking" documented by Roger Abrahams.[21] I am not aware of any term used by the quartet singers themselves to describe this phenomenon.

Singers employ this device when emotions are running high and the program has reached a fever pitch. Its very existence implies a two-way dialogue with an audience that responds with shouts of encouragement such as "Sing it!" or "I feel that spirit!" This powerful point in the performance involves both the audience and the quartets in a heated spiritual exchange called "getting happy," "shouting," or "feeling the spirit." Neither party is a mere recipient or a transitive agent; both take positive, forceful, and direct roles in this two-way line of communication. It is an intensely moving experience that helps sweep both the singers and their audience onto a more advanced emotional plane. Such a dialogue resembles the keen emotional lift that can be created in a tightly packed basketball arena as the crowd and the home team feed off one another.

The gospel quartet audience shows its approval and participates in other ways, too. The people often clap more loudly for specific quartets or request an encore. And because they are familiar with the quartets and their music, they frequently call out for certain musical selections and acknowledge some of the more impressive vocal techniques or choreography displayed on stage. These are just a few of the ways the audience becomes an indispensable part of the performance.

The three agents in these gospel events know their parts well, for such public performances have gone on in Memphis since the 1920s. The programs have evolved over the past sixty years into a standardized format, closing with a prayer offered by one of the ministers. This does not mean that the emotions and singing are not heartfelt or real, but the framing devices that signal the beginning and end of a gospel quartet program vary little among performances. Many people come to participate during the singing itself, for this is when everyone enjoys the spontaneity and spirituality. Along with the ritualized opening and closing ceremonies, mutual participation and an understanding of these well-mapped-out roles constitute the very heart of a gospel quartet performance.

The programs themselves, whether local, professional, or a mixture of the two, typically follow the format just described. However, there have been two types of closely related, specialized programs that are a little different in their intent. These are *quartet contests* and *song battles.* Quartet contests simply pit one group against another. Although little has been written on the subject, such contests have been reported in Birmingham, Alabama, and the Virginia Tidewater. During the 1930s and 1940s, churches primarily held the contests in Memphis. They were billed as quartet contests in order to build up greater interest in specific programs, a ploy that often worked. Each group would have to perform between four and six selections and the quartet giving the best performance was declared the victor.

Judges for these contests evaluated the finer aspects of singing and determined the winners by assigning points to each group. Although the criteria were subjective, they usually included rhythmic precision, enunciation of words, inventiveness, accuracy of harmony, and ability of the singers. Judges were almost always quartet singers who were not participating on the program. Elijah Jones, a veteran judge, trainer, and singer, explained the selection process: "I always liked judging 'cause so many folks didn't know singing. You got three judges that know singing, then you get fairly seeded. They would look for time, music, don't miss no minors or sharps. The one that makes the most points, that's the one that wins. During that particular time [1930s], we didn't have but four voices: leader, tenor, baritone, and bass. They would listen to each voice. We had judges all up into the late thirties and forties." [22]

Local sponsoring churches often held such contests to raise money. The winning group received a modest share of the donations collected at the door, but perhaps more important, the group members' performing ability was acknowledged by their peers. To be champion of a quartet contest meant prestige and greater respect for the group, which is one of the reasons why the contests were so popular. During the 1940s and 1950s quartet singing became even more fashionable, and a shift occurred in the format and style of these competitions: they became song battles and were frequently staged in large auditoriums.

In Memphis, many song battles took place in the Mason's Temple or the City Auditorium downtown. These performance events were a manifestation of popular culture and a logical evolution of the earlier contests. The audience's applause, rather than peers intimately familiar with quartet singing, decided the winner of the song battle. Elijah Jones observed, "we started having audiences judging in the '50s [and] then you just get out there hoopin' and hollerin', and if they like that, then you be the man." [23] His obvious disdain for the event reflected a clear movement from a program ruled by the quartets themselves to one dominated by popular opinion. That these competitions had changed is reinforced by Julius Readers: "It sort of worked like the group that get the most shouts or the most applause—you know what the favorite group was. You didn't need judges then because if you were tough, when you hit the floor you knowed who had it then, because two to one if you a favorite in that town, when they call your name, everybody just go wild! Then you get up there, their hands clap, and you know who was the winner." [24]

The fact that large auditoriums were the sites of so many song battles further underscores the movement away from community or neighborhood events and toward a more secular world, in which popular tastes prevailed. Regardless of the context or motivation, some singers did not approve of this emphasis on competitiveness and refused to participate in the song battles. They felt that quartets should work together in their musical ministry and not try to prove one quartet's superiority over others. In their view such performances violated the spirit of fellowship that bound singers together.[25] As interest in quartets dwindled nationwide, in the late 1950s, fewer people turned out for song battles and the number of these programs fell; today they are completely anachronistic.

The final context in which quartets can be observed is their regularly scheduled rehearsals, which are not open to the general public. Like the public programs, however, quartet rehearsals follow a format to which the group rigorously adheres. The opening cue is a prayer and scripture reading by a group member. Then the president calls the roll, reads the minutes from the previous meeting, and asks for discussion of old and new business. The treasurer covers financial matters and the secretary gives an account of upcoming programs. While such business and procedural matters seem mundane, they often take up about one-quarter of each rehearsal. These weekly gatherings, which usually rotate among the homes of each quartet member, provide an arena for the discussion of mutual concerns and are critical for the week-by-week operation of the group. Rehearsals are also important for polishing material, working on older songs, and introducing new tunes or arrangements. If the quartet has a musical advisor or trainer, most of these decisions are left to him. Nearly all of the rehearsals that I attended, however, were remarkably democratic. A spirit of cooperation prevailed, and members were able and often encouraged to volunteer their views regarding the music.

Different singers often have their "own" songs that feature the lead vocal. When rehearsing these numbers, the featured singer would most often make suggestions for changes in tempo, dynamics, or the timing of the background singers. Sometimes one singer would stop and alter the voicings if someone was not following the proper line or if they felt they could improve the harmony. Such alterations were always open to discussion, and in the absence of a recognized trainer the song leader's opinion had priority. The process of learning or reworking material is still an oral tradition and seems to have changed little since the era of Gus Miller and Elijah Jones. The rehearsals themselves last anywhere from one to three hours. When the quartet completes work on singing, the next step is to agree on the time and location for the next meeting. Then a closing prayer is offered and the rehearsal ends.

Quartets in Memphis retain their feeling of an extended family. As the family grows older, its members become more acutely aware of death reducing their numbers. Younger people join the community, permitting groups like the Gospel Writers, the Pattersonaires, and the Spirit of Memphis to thrive. As long as a singer such as the Spirit of Memphis's Earl Malone teaches young singers his distinctive bass lines and the group's repertoire, this unique community will continue to exist and evolve in new directions.[26]

NOTES

1. See Alan Merriam and Raymond Mack, "The Jazz Community," *Social Forces,* 38 (1960), pp. 200–219; Robert Stebbins, "The Jazz Community: The Sociology of a Musical Sub-Culture" (Ph.D. dissertation, University of Minnesota, 1964); Robert Stebbins, "A Theory of the Jazz Community," in *American Music: From Storyville to Woodstock,* ed. Charles Nanry (New Brunswick, N.J.: Transaction Books, 1972), pp. 115–34; William Ferris, *Blues from the Delta* (Garden City, N.Y.: Doubleday, 1979); and Raymond Allen, "Old-Time Music and the Urban Folk Revival," *New York Folklore,* 7 (1981), pp. 65–81.

2. Merriam and Mack, "Jazz Community," p. 211.

3. Ferris, *Blues from the Delta,* p. 22.

4. Doug Seroff, brochure notes, *"Bless My Bones": Memphis Gospel Radio—The 1950s,* Pea-Vine PLP-9051 (Tokyo, 1982), p. 1.

5. Huddie Moore, interviewed by Kip Lornell, February 2, 1983. Unless indicated otherwise, all interviews were conducted by the author in Memphis, Tennessee. A copy of the tapes and a transcript are deposited in the Mississippi Valley Collection, Brister Library, Memphis State University.

6. Mary Davis, interview, May 10, 1982.

7. Cleo Satterfield, interview, June 7, 1982.

8. Moore interview.

9. Etherlene Beans, interview, July 3, 1982.

10. Flozell Leland, interview, June 6, 1982.

11. Beans interview.

12. Jack Miller, interview, October 1980.

13. Beans interview.

14. Leon Moody, interview, February 8, 1981.

15. James Harvey, interview, June 19, 1981.

16. Elijah Jones, interview, October 1979.

17. Willie Neal, interview, April 14, 1981.

18. Tommie Todd, interview, August 11, 1982.

19. Moody interview.

20. For summaries of this concept see Lawrence Levine, *Black Culture and Black Consciousness* (New York: Oxford University Press, 1977), pp. 174–90; see also Portia K. Maultsby, *Afro-American Religious Music: A Study in Musical Diversity* (Springfield, Ohio: The Hymn Society of America, 1980).

21. Roger Abrahams, "The Training of Man-of-Words in Talking Sweet," in *The Man-of-Words in the West Indies* (Baltimore: Johns Hopkins University Press, 1984), pp. 109–21.

22. Jones interview.

23. Ibid.

24. Julius Readers, interview, May 28, 1982.

25. For a different perspective on song battles see Burt Feintuck, "A Noncommercial Black Gospel Group in Context: We Live the Life We Sing About," in *Black Music Research Journal,* 1 (1980), pp. 37–50.

26. Ray Allen discusses this aspect of the music, as well as gospel singing as a complex performance event, in "'Singing in the Spirit': An Ethnography of Gospel Performance in New York City's African American Community" (Ph.D. dissertation, University of Pennsylvania, 1987).

CHAPTER

5

"On Records and over
the Airwaves"

Commercial radio stations and record companies always try to give their audiences what they think is or will be in line with popular tastes. But popular tastes are notoriously fickle. The commercial success of most musicians is fleeting at best, which is why the mass media are always looking for something new.

Until the post–World War II years, most of Memphis's black gospel quartets sang in neighborhood churches and remained closely allied with the folk community. This situation changed quickly after the war, however, when thousands of fans regularly packed the Mason's Temple and the City Auditorium for programs featuring professional quartets. As the popularity of black gospel quartet music grew in Memphis, the relationships among local groups, radio stations, and record companies became stronger. This symbiotic association reached its zenith between 1950 and 1955, when Peacock/Duke Records was recording the most popular Memphis quartets and radio stations like WDIA broadcast "live" performances by many Memphis groups. However, such business affiliations actually began some twenty-five years earlier.

Near the turn of the century the commercial recording of traditional music in America began with companies like Victor and Columbia issuing performances of indigenous folk and ethnic musicians. Not until the early 1920s did the recorded documentation of American folk music reach significant proportions. During that decade and the next, thousands of black jazz bands, hillbilly singers, gospel groups, blues musicians, and string bands made records.[1] Memphis gospel quartets also played a small part in the pre–World War II recording boom.

The first and only local group documented during this era was the I.C. Glee Club, which OKeh Records brought into its temporary Memphis studio on February 16, 1928. Employees of the Illinois Central Railroad founded this group—one of at least three Memphis area quartets to bear the initials "I.C." Although OKeh did not release a single song from this initial session (possibly because of technical problems), the group traveled to Atlanta a year later to record six more sides for the company, all of which were issued. The group continued to record for OKeh until their final session in 1930 in New York City, which yielded four records.[2]

Such spatial variation in recording sites was not unusual, because OKeh and other record companies regularly sent portable field units to cities across the South, where they remained for several days to three weeks. Memphis, Atlanta, New Orleans, San Antonio, and St. Louis were just some of the locations in which OKeh recorded during the late 1920s. In addition to the I.C. Glee Club, the company recorded only one other Mid-South quartet while in Memphis in 1928; the Invincible Quartet of Rust College, located about fifty miles southeast of Memphis in Holly Springs, Mississippi. OKeh also documented blues singers during this session, two of whom, Lonnie Johnson and John Hurt, were to become well-known.

These field recording sessions were always arranged in advance. Some of the musicians had previously recorded, but the companies were always seeking new talent. Sometimes they followed the advice of their own record dealers; in other cases they relied on the expertise of local singers. Two black bandleaders in Memphis, Will Shade and Fess Williams, were intimately familiar with local blues and jazz performers and almost certainly "scouted" for previously unrecorded talent, asking them to attend the sessions.[3]

After this early OKeh session with the I.C. Glee Club, no other Memphis gospel quartet recorded for nearly twenty years. There are two probable reasons for this long hiatus. First, the Great Depression pushed most record companies into or near bankruptcy. A very few companies, like Columbia, that went bankrupt were quickly reorganized and struggled through the 1930s. They never recorded any Memphis quartets, however, preferring instead to stay with predepression artists like Charley Patton, Willie McTell, Rev. J. M. Gates, and the Norfolk Jubilee Quartet. The inherently conservative nature of these companies, which became even more evident as the industry began recovering during the mid- to late 1930s, also hindered the chances for Memphis groups to record. The quartets that did record during the few years prior to World War II—the Heavenly Gospel Singers, the Golden Gate Quartet, and Mitchell's Christian Singers—tended to be either well established or groups whose initial records sold well. The other major reason that no Memphis quartets made records during this period was that few companies conducted field recording sessions after 1930 and almost none were held in the Mid-South. The American Record Corporation, for instance, held the only Memphis field session in 1939 and they recorded no black religious music.

After World War II the very nature of the record industry changed. Between 1942 and late 1944 shortages of the shellac necessary to press records, along with a recording ban called by the American Federation of Musicians, very effectively shut down the entire industry. As the war finally ground to a close and America's economy began to recover, a new spirit of entrepreneurship in the record business became evident. Columbia and Victor and their related companies tended to dominate the industry prior to 1945, but the late 1940s witnessed a rapid proliferation of small record companies that were willing to take a risk on local or regional talent of every conceivable description.

There are many obscure and important examples of this phenomenon from all over the country. In New York City, Atlantic Records and Apollo Records each entered the market and made a significant impact by issuing a wide variety of folk, popular, and jazz discs. Chicago was home base for the Aristocrat/Chess complex of labels, while Los Angeles served as headquarters for Imperial Records. In Memphis, Sam Phillips's Sun label became a critical force in recording rockabilly and rhythm 'n' blues music but had little impact on religious music.[4] There were scores of other companies located in smaller cities and rural areas across the United States, though many released only a few records before folding. The fact is that although literally hundreds of independent record companies formed after 1945, only a minute fraction of them became successful business enterprises. Yet they did record numerous fascinating and important examples of American music. And as a result of this trend, more Memphis groups finally gained access to the recording studios.

The first local group to get into the studio during this entrepreneurial period was the Spirit of Memphis. The group's experience clearly illustrates how these new record companies operated and also demonstrates the importance of professionalism among quartets, another important aspect of gospel singing during the immediate postwar years. Throughout the 1940s the Spirit of Memphis was perhaps the most popular quartet in the Mid-South. Although each of the singers maintained a full-time job, the group sang nearly every weekend and on local programs during the week. The weekend engagements frequently carried the group far from Memphis, and it was at one of these out-of-town programs that the group got its break.

The year was 1948 and the Spirit of Memphis had been engaged to sing in Birmingham, Alabama, on a major program. Robert Reed recalls the trip:

> We sang this song, "Happy in the Service of the Lord." And the audience, I don't know what happened, but they . . . acted like they hadn't heard a song like that before. It just went over big! So this guy, this nice white guy, so he said, "How would you guys like to record that song for me?" We said, "Okay," you know. He was the director of this radio station. . . . It was in Bessemer, a very popular station there. We sang this song down there at the auditorium and the promoter was a guy named Polk. So when we got the engagement there, then he, Mr. Polk, asked us how would we like to record "Happy in the Service of the Lord?" And do you know that we recorded that record and we couldn't keep 'em there in Birmingham![5]

It is not clear exactly what company first issued the record. The entry for the selection in Cedrick Hayes and Robert Laughton's discography credits the issue to De Luxe,[6] an independent company based in New Jersey. There is an advertisement in the June 14, 1949, *Memphis World,* however, listing the Spirit of Memphis as Hallelujah Record Company artists. Quartet members Robert Reed and Earl Malone recall selling the record locally before it was available on De Luxe.[7] Thus it appears that Hallelujah was probably a "one-shot" label that Polk produced and the group marketed;

later a deal was worked out with De Luxe, and by late 1949 the New Jersey-based company was marketing the disc. In any event, this recording of "I'm Happy in the Service of the Lord" set the local gospel community ablaze. Besides capturing a fine performance, the record symbolized the acceptance of Memphis quartet singing by a larger and more far-flung audience. It was almost certainly on the strength of this record and its well-deserved local and regional reputation that the Spirit of Memphis reached an agreement with King Records—one of the larger and more important independent companies.

King Records is an archetype for all postwar independent enterprises. Formed by Syd Nathan in 1943, King built a strong, diverse catalog that included hillbilly artists like the Delmore Brothers and the Brown's Ferry Four, as well as popular black artists like Tiny Bradshaw and the Swan Silvertone Singers. Nathan seemed especially drawn to black gospel music and the money it brought to his company. By late 1949 the Spirit of Memphis had signed an exclusive agreement with King Records and remained with the company until the close of 1952—halcyon years when their base of popularity was solid. The group's live performances were outstanding, with a lineup that featured the powerful, often breathtaking alternating leads by Wilbur "Little Ax" Broadnax, Silas Steele, and Jethroe Bledsoe.

"Jet" Bledsoe, an early member of the Spirit of Memphis, still lives in Memphis. He vividly recalls when the quartet was on top:

> "Days Past and Gone" was the record that really introduced us on King Records. Silas Steele was preaching on that record. Nobody had ever heard anything like that! We got that record out there . . . and that's what sold us throughout the country. Silas was a great singer and a showman. He was second lead and he would "brace" me anytime we would get in tight 'cause he could talk. That's when we had some of them talking records. They criticized me for letting him do that type of thing on a record, 'cause nobody wasn't doing no preaching when I made the record "Lord, Jesus." They [King Records] caught it in the auditorium [the Mason's Temple]. He [Syd Nathan] put that thing out and that record went out all over everywhere! We made all kinds of money and that's the way we got to go on the road and make appearances. We would pack every auditorium everywhere! Sometimes I look at the map up there [of the United States] and I say, "Well, which states haven't I been in?"[8]

Besides the aforementioned "preaching" records, the Spirit of Memphis recorded quite a few jubilee-style arrangements of traditional songs like "I'm on the Battlefield" and "Everytime I Feel the Spirit." The group also delved into more contemporary gospel material. One of the best examples of this is "The Atomic Telephone," which incorporates the once-popular "atomic age" motif with the somewhat more traditional theme of communicating with Jesus by way of the telephone. Such vivid imagery, a wonderful example of popular songwriting, apparently came from the pen of Syd Nathan. "The Atomic Telephone" is not an anomaly; several artists, including other religious singers, recorded songs using this theme.[9]

Although its King recordings sold well, the Spirit of Memphis soon grew dissatisfied with the financial arrangements. According to Earl Malone, a lack of accountability and perhaps honesty were the prime reasons the quartet and King Records parted ways late in 1952: ". . . he'd [Nathan] give us an advance, an advance royalty. And . . . that was the size of it. He'd give us maybe $400 or $500 . . . to cut a session. We never did get no statement."[10] Shortly thereafter the Spirit of Memphis signed with the aggressive and tough Don Robey of Peacock Records, thus beginning an association that lasted until the late 1960s.

Earl Malone recalls that Robey offered the group a respectable financial arrangement and even traveled to Memphis from Houston to sign the contract. By contrast, record companies in postwar Memphis all but ignored local quartets. Even Sam Phillips, the city's most talented record entrepreneur, whose reputation as a hustler with an eye for talent was well deserved, evidently believed that such groups did not have enough commercial potential—or maybe he was too busy trying to deal with the likes of Carl Perkins, Elvis Presley, Rufus Thomas, Joe Hill Louis, Jr. Parker, and Jerry Lee Lewis. Phillips did record four local quartets—the Gospel Tones, the Brewsteraires, the Gospel Travelers, and the Southern Jubilees—but he released virtually none of their sides. Chess picked up and issued one Brewsteraires disc, and Sun released one record each by Brother James Anderson and the Jones Brothers (the latter two are stylistically removed from the quartet tradition). For the most part, however, companies outside the Mid-South provided Memphis quartets with recording opportunities. Robey was in charge of the Peacock and Duke labels, which recorded the majority of Memphis gospel quartet sides (fifty-two of ninety) during the 1950s. He had the Spirit of Memphis under contract between 1953 and 1968, while the Sunset Travelers and the Southern Wonders had much briefer, though earlier associations with his companies. (According to matrix numbers assigned for the Southern Wonders' initial session, it was the first group to record for Robey.)

He certainly made money with gospel quartets or he would not have recorded so many of them. Because Duke/Peacock was a very small operation with only a handful of people involved in its day-to-day business operations, the singers themselves had extensive personal contact with Robey. Their opinions of him vary, but by all accounts he was an extremely demanding person, a perfectionist with a clear vision of what he wanted. Grover Blake, founder and manager of the Sunset Travelers, perhaps best describes Robey: "If you trying to get *his* ideas, he was 100 percent with you."[11]

If Blake and the Sunset Travelers were wary and respectful of Don Robey, the same could not be said for Jack Franklin and the Southern Wonders. Robey's suggestion that the Southern Wonders sing popular music in addition to religious songs antagonized the quartet. Ernest Moore, a group member between 1952 and 1957, reflects on the increasingly hostile situation: Robey "was an uncooperative man. He knew what would sell, he wouldn't let us record it. First thing he wanted us to sing pop and we wouldn't sing it. What was the song, 'Lovie Dovie'? That's what he wanted us to sing. When it came to gospel music, he thought he could lure you over to sing what he wanted you to sing."[12] The Southern Wonders' manager and founder, Jack Franklin, echoes Moore's observations: "He dragged me out to see his fishing boat and that's where he wanted to talk all that stuff [singing secular music]. What Robey cared about gospel music and religion wasn't nothing! He was a millionaire and he was making money. At that time pop would sell fast. He was trying to get Blair and McKinney . . . have Blair play pop and have McKinney sing 'em."[13]

This bickering and Robey's attempt to factionalize the Southern Wonders escalated to such a level that the group attempted to break their contract with him. This proved impossible because Robey's hold over them included more than juat a recording relationship: he was also the owner of the Buffalo Booking Agency of Houston, Texas, the exclusive agent for live performance dates by

Peacock/Duke artists. In addition to refusing to release the Southern Wonders from their recording contract, Robey also placed a stranglehold on their touring schedule. Jack Franklin explains:

> One thing we did, we refused to take any more bookings. We just stopped and told Evelyn [Johnson, secretary of the Buffalo Booking Agency] that if she didn't book the places closer together, we just weren't gonna do it! She had us booked in Pensacola, and had us jumping from Florida to Grand Rapids, Michigan! She had started booking them close together, 100 to 200 miles apart, but that trip was a little too far apart.[14]

The Southern Wonders made no more recordings after their final Peacock session in mid-1953, yet they did stay together as a full-time professional quartet until late 1957, when they finally came off the road to resettle in Memphis. Unquestionably, some bitterness toward Don Robey remains in the hearts of at least several of the group members, but this is tempered by an understanding of his importance in furthering their careers.

Although Grover Blake staunchly maintains that he and the Sunset Travelers kept on Don Robey's good side, there appears to have been some ill-will between them regarding singer O. V. Wright. During the early 1950s Wright was a high school student in suburban Germantown, Tennessee, when Blake recruited him. Wright was one of the superb quartet singers of the 1950s and performed with the Sunset Travelers for several years. In 1956 he left Blake's group to join the ever-popular Spirit of Memphis. Two years later Wright left gospel music altogether, lured by Don Robey's promises of a career in pop music. Wright never returned to religious singing, a fact that seemed to upset Grover Blake, though he never directly stated it.

A similar situation occurred with Joe Hinton at roughly the same time. Hinton was a dynamic lead singer with the Spirit of Memphis in 1957 and 1958, but he left the group after listening to Robey's popular music pitch. Earl Malone relates:

> He was with us for a good while until Robey, you know, talked to him about everything he could do with the pop field. Robey talked him into it, you know what I mean. He and I was roommates . . . out on the road. And he talked to me about it. I said, "Well, if you think you can do better—do it!" So he decided he'd better get started . . .

Robey was interested in him . . . thought he would make another Sam Cooke.[15]

At the root of these conflicts seems to have been the need to reconcile religious convictions with the more lucrative financial rewards offered in the popular music field. Gospel quartet singers frequently were torn between serving the Lord through song and the prospects of more comfortable circumstances in the popular sector. But despite the temptation, the overwhelming majority of singers and quartets in Memphis remained with religious music. Former gospel disc jockey and quartet singer Eugene Walton has very strong opinions on this subject:

> I'm a firm believer that to be successful, you have to pick which way you want to go and go that way. Our [the Gospel Travelers'] deter-mination was to stick with gospel. In the black audience, they won't tolerate it here in Memphis—you singing blues and gospel all at the same time. They won't accept it. We didn't go [into pop music] be-cause we would have been committing suicide in gospel. Above that, my religious belief is that . . . whatever you going to do, you do it. But don't straddle the fence.[16]

Regardless of these webs of conflict and the problems between Robey and the Memphis quartet singers, his documentation of this music is unparalleled. Whether some other regional record entre-preneur, such as Johnny Vincent of Ace Records in Jackson, Missis-sippi, would have taken the initiative to record these Memphis quartets remains pure speculation. David Clark, who worked as a producer and an artists and repertoire (A&R) man for Peacock/Duke Records between 1953 and 1970, provides an inside view of Robey and the way he ran his business.[17] Clark, who today does A&R work for Malaco Records in Jackson, Mississippi, produced dozens of jazz, blues, gospel, and pop sessions for Robey and, along with his boss and Evelyn Johnson, was at the heart of the com-pany's operation in Houston and later in New York City.

> I think Robey was one of the most controversial guys ever been in the business. I worked with Robey for eighteen years. For eighteen years I got my money on time. . . . He did some great things for me and some great things for the groups. A lot of the groups, I'm going to tell you what happened, especially with gospel groups. They'd go down to Houston; they'd go to Robey's office. "We need a

car." Robey would buy them a car. "We need $10,000 for uniforms." Robey would buy them uniforms. Robey would have them sign for their money. This was Robey's money, it wasn't theirs! Robey would have them sign a promissory note. Now when royalty time come, and time to collect his money, the groups would freeze up because they figure they shouldn't have to pay it all at once. They wanted royalties, but they had gotten their money up front, and Robey was going to get his. It was that simple.[18]

Robey was, according to Clark, an extremely shrewd business-man, with the record company and booking agency being only two of his many ventures. Although he kept himself well informed and was intimately involved with the daily operation of his musical entrepreises, Robey was also deeply embroiled in financial matters totally unrelated to music:

Most of the time Robey was watching his horses—his other invest-ment. Robey had a lot of investments. Robey also had about thirty or forty of his own racehorses. What made him so controversial, no-body ever knew what he was doing. A lot of them rock and roll groups that was appearing across the country . . . part of the bank-roll was from Robey. Alan Freed did a lot of things with Robey's money. He could go through a lot of money. Robey was a gambler. Robey was the only gambler, I think the only man I knew, could walk around with a million dollars in his pocket and nobody would rob him![19]

One of the more interesting recordings from this era, "God's Chariot" (Parts 1 and 2), indirectly involves Don Robey. The year was 1952 and the Gospel Travelers were singing regularly over WDIA. David Mattis, one of the station administrators, decided that the time was right to enter the growing field of independent record companies. He heard the group sing a topical song one day, quickly decided that this song had commercial potential, and chose it to kick off his new Duke label: "They had a great tornado that went through the Mid-South and this bunch called the Gospel Travelers came up and they wanted to cut it and we cut it as a two-sided record and I cut the wind behind it and 'God's Chariot' was the tornado. It was a really exciting gospel thing. . . . It was excit-ing with the wind and the tornado came and God came roaring across the field."[20]

Because he was new in the business, Mattis was soon seeking a partner with more savvy and record industry connections. After sifting through his options, he signed a contract with Don Robey in the fall of 1952. Like so many people before and after him, Mattis soon had ill feelings about his new business associate; not surprisingly, money was involved. When Mattis confronted Robey, the Houston businessman pulled out a .45-caliber revolver and placed in on the desk. After a prolonged negotiation that involved many dollars in legal fees and a good deal of bitterness, the two men reached a settlement. In the end Mattis got some cash, copyright agreements, and future royalties, while Robey ended up with some fine master tapes, which would eventually make money for him, as well as rights to the Duke label.[21]

Of course, Robey did not record all of the best quartets in Memphis or even all of the "commercial" groups, but his impact was the most profound. Nashboro Records in Nashville, Tennessee, recorded many regional black gospel groups, though they were involved with only two Memphis quartets: the Dixie Nightingales and the Sons of Jehovah. This brief association occurred in 1959 and 1960, at the end of the period when quartets were popular. As a result of this neglect, gospel quartets in Memphis largely turned to "vanity" record labels. Such companies provide local quartets, or anyone else with enough money, with a 45-rpm disc or an LP album they can sell. The group pays a set fee for the studio time and the cost of labels, sleeves, and pressing; and the studio owner turns over the 500 or 1,000 records to the group, whose responsibility it is to market them. The profit for studio owners comes from their role as middlemen: they generally bill their clients about 25 percent above costs.

Style Wooten's Designer, Good News, and Golden Rule imprints comprise the most active vanity labels used by Memphis gospel groups since the late 1960s. Although Wooten has been in the record business only since 1968, precise information regarding his various labels is difficult to obtain. It appears, however, that he has recorded at least two local quartets—the Harps of Melody and the Royal Harmony Four. One of the first groups with which Wooten worked in the late 1960s was the Harps of Melody, and since this was also one of the Designer label's first releases, he recalls the session vividly: "It was like this . . . it was something new. If you gonna be in the record business, you have to adapt. I adapted. You gotta get in there and work with it. I used Charles Bourne [on piano] . . . to try and hold them on key and give them something for the station to play. I didn't know whether the station would play it or not. It was a new experience trying to work with them, to be the best possible, always keeping in mind airplay." [22]

Several other local quartets that generally sang a cappella also experienced an augmentation of their ranks when they went into the studio. Flozell Leland of the Millerettes recalls that her group did a session with J & W Records, a very obscure Memphis company that issued a handful of records in the mid-1960s before going out of business: "I felt like . . . we could do the job without music [instruments], but they felt that we couldn't do the job without music. This led us to . . . believe that they knew what they were doing. Maybe they did and maybe they didn't; anyway, they stuck this music to us." [23]

Most recently, High Water Records, which is affiliated with Memphis State University, entered the field of black gospel quartet music. In 1983 the company issued two 45-rpm discs by two male quartets and a long-playing anthology of Memphis quartets (see the Prelude and Appendix II). More recently the same label has released two albums by local harmony gospel groups, the Pattersonaires and the venerable Spirit of Memphis. It remains to be seen whether specialist labels like High Water will continue to document this music or whether private entrepreneurs in the spirit of Don Robey will move back into this field of recording.

Several Memphis radio stations have provided a significant forum for black gospel quartets equal in importance to the role that the record companies played. Although quartet performances on local radio can be documented as early as 1929, they did not assume a prominent role until the late 1940s when KWEM and WDIA featured regularly scheduled "live" broadcasts. The importance of these broadcasts for Memphis quartets cannot be overstated. They served the dual purpose of promoting the group's musical ministry and the quartet itself. Radio instantly provided quartets with a larger and more far-flung audience than they could possibly hope to reach at any local church. Singers quickly recognized the importance of radio and, as Huddie Moore of the Spiritual Four explains, its almost magical power to expand their audience: "It was pretty important. . . . [Say] you was going to have a program on Sunday evening; when you do your broadcast, you announce where you going to be, name of the church and who's going to be on your program to help you. It will help to sell your crowd for the program."[24]

Like many Memphis quartets, the Spiritual Four, which Moore founded in the late 1930s, sang over at least three local radio stations between the late 1940s and the mid-1960s. The group had a regular weekly program on WDIA during the early 1950s, followed by a similar stint on KWAM, and completed its radio career with broadcasts on WLOK in 1964. This pattern is typical of quartet radio work and represents a trend that began near the dawn of radio broadcasting in Memphis.

As well as being the first Memphis group to record, the I.C. Glee Club holds a similar distinction in the field of broadcasting. Probably because of OKeh's interest, WREC invited the group to their studios. The *Memphis Press-Scimitar* of February 1, 1929, offers the following information: "The feature from WREC, 'Voice of Memphis Station,' Friday-night will be the singing of the I.C. Glee Club Negro quartet. These harmony singers have been heard in many leading cities in the North and East, and have made numerous tours. They will be on the air from 8 to 9:00 PM."[25] According to officials of the Illinois Central Gulf Railroad, this was the quartet's second appearance on WREC; the theme of their program "was built around an imaginary trip on ICRR's Memphis-St. Louis 'Chickasaw' passenger train."[26] From this description it would appear that OKeh Records recorded the theme song either under the title "Panama to Chi" or "I'm Going Home on the Chickasaw Train."

According to interviews with local quartet singers, we know that at least the following groups had radio programs: the Spirit of Memphis, the Gospel Travelers, the Four Stars of Harmony, the I.C. Hummingbirds, and the Independent Quartet. These live shows were heard over WHBQ, WMPS, WMC, and WNRB (which is no longer in business). And there were certainly other gospel quartets performing on Memphis radio stations during the depression years.

The increased number of black quartet appearances on Memphis radio clearly parallels popular interest in this music and its documentation by record companies. Many more Memphis quartets broadcast regularly during the 1940s and 1950s than during the 1930s. Unquestionably, two stations (WDIA and KWEM) played the paramount role in promoting and disseminating quartet music over the Mid-South's airwaves. KWEM began serving the area from West Memphis, Arkansas, in 1946 with a format that blended secular and religious music, news, and talk shows, most of which were oriented toward a white audience. The sizable Afro-American population in Memphis was clearly underserved by the mass media, however, and by 1949 KWEM had altered its policies in an attempt to reach this market. Their strategy was to add a few black disc jockeys and to expand their programming of black secular and sacred music. Several very important rhythm 'n' blues artists of the 1950s and 1960s broadcast over this station early in their careers: Jr. Parker, James Cotton, and Howlin' Wolf (Chester Burnett). Howlin' Wolf, for example, had a weekly program on KWEM in 1952, just about the time his recordings for RPM and Chess hit the market. Black gospel music also entered the station's format at about the same time.

Although KWEM programmed black gospel music throughout the day, the station confined this music primarily to Sunday morning. Before KWEM moved its studios to Memphis and altered its call letters to KWAM in 1953, many local quartets traveled across the Mississippi River Bridge to perform on these Sunday morning broadcasts. Walter Stewart, a black man who served as a liaison between the station and the groups, was the first emcee for the Sunday morning broadcasts. The quartets that appeared are known to include the Jollyaires (to which Stewart belonged), the Southern Jubilees, the Evening Doves, the Harps of Melody, the Gospel Travelers, and the Keystone Masters of Harmony.

The only change made when these Sunday morning programs moved to Memphis was that "Cousin" Eugene Walton took over Walter Stewart's position. Cousin Eugene, of the Gospel Travelers, maintained his dual role as disc jockey and quartet singer until his group disbanded in the middle 1960s. He continued to work at the station, however, until his retirement in 1982, after nearly thirty years of service. Walton's retirement resulted from policy disagreements with management and a format shift that relegated gospel music to a much less prominent role.

Cousin Eugene's affiliation with local quartets was most important during the 1950s when the station regularly played and heavily promoted this music:

> Mostly on Sunday mornings the various groups had broadcasts on the station. I was the only one they chose to be the emcee on the air. The station's responsibility was for booking the groups and, of course, it was my responsibility to see that they got on the air on time. I made the various announcements and made sure everything went right. The groups started coming on at 7:00 A.M. . . . right up until 10:00 or 10:30 A.M. Most likely they had a 15-minute program each, but every once in a while some had a 30-minute show. Mostly, the groups sponsored their own selves. I don't think many of them had an outside sponsor.[27]

The cost of airtime during the early 1950s was about twelve dollars per quarter hour, and most quartets willingly paid this fee because of the publicity the broadcasts brought to them. Only a very small percentage of the Memphis groups had records available, making radio their most important medium for exposure. Walton relates:

> Well, they wanted to be heard. Some of the groups think they sing very well and the people didn't know about them. That was their way of getting heard . . . getting on the air so people could hear them. And by the same token, the people listened to them on the air. That's how they got established. If you weren't on the air, you had a pretty rough go with trying to get programs. That was why it was vitally important to be on the air.[28]

After a half-year of experience with these live Sunday broadcasts, Cousin Eugene slowly began to accept more duties at KWAM. He soon hosted a two-hour Saturday afternoon shift featuring records by the Trumpeteers, the Jubilaires, the Golden Gate Quartet, the Dixie Hummingbirds, and other popular quartets. Within a year after his first air-shift, Walton was a full-time employee of KWAM.

KWAM's weekly schedule featured live quartet programming until the late 1950s; by 1960 it had entirely ceased. This radical shift occurred for two major reasons. First, popular tastes moved away from the quartets and toward other forms of black gospel music. Second, KWAM's management changed its financial and managerial policies. Walton recalls that "the gospel format opened up and we began to take in church services, so that kind of narrowed the time for quartets because church services mostly want a whole hour. We had so many demands for church services that it limited the time for quartets. The church naturally had their listening audiences . . . [and] could also pay more money."[29]

KWAM's switch to other programming enabled WDIA to become an even more consequential outlet for Memphis gospel music and quartets. WDIA began as a low-power daytime operation in 1948, and from its inception the station oriented itself toward a black audience. During its first few years, WDIA programmed much religious music. Rev. W. Herbert Brewster's renowned "Camp Meeting of the Air," a show that spotlighted many local gospel singers like Queen C. Anderson and the Brewsteraires, was broadcast live on WDIA. In fact, many of the best local black religious groups sang on this station at one time.[30]

The impact and critical importance of WDIA increased dramatically in July 1954 when the station boosted its power to the maximum permissible output of 50,000 watts and began around-the-clock programming. Prior to this time the station served only Memphis and the immediate surrounding counties. The changes meant that WDIA virtually blanketed the Mid-South, as well as many other sections of the country after sundown. Thus WDIA instantly became the primary outlet for ambitious black quartets because they now could reach hundreds of thousands of people.

Even before this power increase, however, WDIA had been a potent force within the community of black musicians in Memphis. Doug Seroff states:

> WDIA was Memphis' premier black music radio station during the legendary years of the early 1950s when the Memphis music scene was exploding with creative energy. At the time the station featured a great deal of live music from their studio. Along with the gospel artists many well known blues and R & B stars, including B. B. King, Johnny Ace and Joe Hill Louis, had regular fifteen-minute programs on WDIA, either weekly or daily. Some of these programs were commercially sponsored, others sponsored by the groups themselves.[31]

There were several notable local and national sponsors for Memphis quartets who broadcast over WDIA. Locally, the Littlejohn Taxi Company was one of the Spirit of Memphis's first sponsors;

General Mills later underwrote this group, while the Pet Milk Company sponsored the Southern Wonders. According to Ford Nelson, an employee of WDIA from 1949 through 1984:

> . . . as far as sponsors are concerned, that would always originate with our sales department. A lot of people didn't know that. We never charged groups to be on the air. If we thought enough of them to put them on the air, we treated them in a special way. If they carved out a big chunk of audience, the sales people would say, "These guys are pretty good." We would cut an audition with a group, say a 15-minute audition with the Dixie Nightingales with my voice on it . . . [if we were] trying to sell it to a sponsor. That made it more professional, rather than a group coming in with Joe's Shine Parlor or something like that. It always gave the station a lot of class.[32]

At the very heart of this activity were two long-time WDIA employees, Theo "Bless My Bones" Wade and Ford Nelson. Wade, who died in 1980, was for many years associated with the Spirit of Memphis prior to joining WDIA's staff and, because of his various affiliations, was one of the key figures in the city's gospel community. Wade did not simply confine himself to his job with WDIA, which began in 1952; he also booked, promoted, and emceed gospel shows. But even more important, members of local quartets had a strong regard for Wade, who seemed to get along with everyone. Nina Jai Daugherty of the Brewster Singers remembers: "Brother Wade was a marvelous person. He was a friend to those quartet singers, gospel singers. He was a good friend to them. He tried to help publicize wherever they were going to be and invite you to be with them. He was simply a great personality."[33]

Theo Wade remained with WDIA until his death. Throughout a nearly thirty-year tenure at the station, his principal role was with religious music. During the week he and Ford Nelson divided a two-hour evening shift entitled "Hallelujah Jubilee," a program devoted to all forms of black gospel music. Each afternoon Nelson had his own show, "The Gospel Train," which also spotlighted the recordings of black gospel groups. The popularity of quartets was such that in 1954 the King Cotton and Nat Buren Packing companies underwrote a daily fifteen-minute program featuring the records of the Golden Gate Quartet.

Interspersed throughout the radio programming day were fifteen- and thirty-minute blocks of live music. Naturally, gospel quartets played a prominent role on these shows. For example, during June 1952, WDIA's daily format included live broadcasts by the Spirit of Memphis (10:00 A.M.–10:15 A.M., sponsored by Gold Medal Flour) and the Songbirds of the South (noon–12:15 P.M., sponsored by the Ballard Company). The same month's Sunday lineup featured a fifteen-minute show by the Gospel Travelers. Such live presentations continued throughout the 1950s, and in 1955 WDIA added a Saturday night program: "Brother Wade had a Saturday-night slot which was something else, which really became an opportunity to showcase a lot of local talent. I wasn't on Saturday nights; he had the whole thing from 7 to 9. It was called 'Hallelujah Jubilee,' . . . [and] about 80 percent to 90 percent was . . . quartets."[34] It was partially through this important program that groups like the Dixie Nightingales, the Sons of Jehovah, the Jordan Wonders, the Jubilee Hummingbirds, the Dixie Wonders, and other "hard" gospel quartets became so popular in the Mid-South.

Another of the quartet-related activities in which WDIA participated was the promotion of concerts throughout the Mid-South. Ford Nelson or Theo Wade emceed many of these programs, which featured groups heard on WDIA. Even more important than these gospel shows were the programs promoted by the station itself. The best known of these was named after one of WDIA's most popular weekly events, "Hallelujah Jubilee Caravan." This name provided a direct connection with WDIA, which helped to attract audiences to the programs. Ford Nelson recalls:

> The station would lease a bus. They would do this about once a month and make contact with some well-known auditorium or . . . hall, maybe down in Mississippi or up in Tennessee. The prime groups would perform on these live shows. We would pick them up and take them on the bus. We would fix up a box of barbecue and have lots of fun! Wade and I would go down and emcee this live show. They would tape it sometimes and bring it back and play it on the air. The shows were . . . very popular with the community.[35]

One of the most widely traveled veterans of Memphis quartet singing, James Darling, thought that Theo Wade was one of the finest emcees in the business:

He turned out to be one of the best in the country, everybody liked him. He was funny, you know . . . had a way of handling his audience. When we were going someplace and the audience seemed to be a little dry . . . he'd walk out casually, unconcerned like. He'd say "I'll tell you what I'd like you to do with me children. We gonna pull a train. I want you to put your hands together. Everytime I do this [claps his hands together], I want you to do it." Like a locomotive. He'd do . . . this and they started faster and faster. At the end he'd say "You sure do burn me out!" That would get the house, you know. We'd have lots of fun off Wade.[36]

The "Star-lite Revue" and the "Goodwill Revue," both WDIA-sponsored, comprised a second type of program. The station produced these programs twice a year—once in the spring and again in the fall—to raise money for crippled black children in Memphis. During the 1950s these revues were divided into two distinct segments: one that featured religious music and another that highlighted popular music. The "Goodwill Revue" of December 4, 1954, provides an example of the caliber of talent these shows attracted. Two of the leading blues performers of the day, Eddie Boyd and Little Walter, headlined the pop music portion. The gospel segment spotlighted two local, albeit very talented, groups—the Spirit of Memphis and the Southern Wonders. Ellis Auditorium was the site for this program and, according to the December 7, 1954, edition of the *Tri-State Defender,* the station raised nearly $7,000.

It is evident from all the primary data that WDIA worked extensively with four or five local quartets, much to the benefit of all parties. While the quartets received the exposure that only this powerful station could provide, WDIA gained community support and added advertising revenues. The support of WDIA ultimately brought the Southern Wonders, the Spirit of Memphis, the Dixie Nightingales, the Songbirds of the South, and the Sunset Travelers all the work they could handle, but ironically it also caused conflicts with the groups' radio broadcasts. Some of them responded by dropping their radio commitments; others reduced the number of broadcasts. Most stations turned to transcriptions, which were prerecorded programs on discs. Doug Seroff observes that the stations routinely recorded transcriptions for broadcast at the appropriate times: "While the artists were in the studio the disc jockeys and engineers sometimes recorded ten-inch vinyl dubs of their most popular numbers, which were played on the air between 'live' broadcasts. Some of the songs on these dubs became better known around Memphis than the artists' recordings."[37] These transcriptions, in fact, are the only sound documents that remain of some quartets. For example, the highly regarded Songbirds of the South never recorded commercially, but several of their 1952 and 1953 transcriptions from WDIA have survived.[38]

As I noted earlier, the general interest in black gospel quartets began to wane in the late 1950s—a trend reflected in local radio programming. By the early 1960s, gospel quartets rarely performed live on either KWAM or WDIA. As long as quartets remained popular, drew crowds, and sold records, they were heard over Memphis's airwaves, but as their popularity diminished, so did their airtime. Today quartet harmony singing is very hard to find on Memphis radio. As far as the local commercial radio programmers are concerned, it is an anachronism. WLOK and WDIA occasionally program records by local quartets like the Spirit of Memphis or nationally recognized groups like the Sensational Nightingales and the Mighty Clouds of Joy. Quartet singing is still appreciated by middle-aged and elderly black residents of Memphis, but because the industry is so oriented toward music that attracts a mass audience, rich gospel harmony singing is not likely to return to Memphis's high-power commercial radio outlets any time soon.

NOTES

1. Useful information on this era is found in Ronald C. Foreman, Jr., "Jazz and Race Records, 1920–1932" (Ph.D. dissertation, University of Illinois, 1968); Robert M. W. Dixon and John Godrich, *Recording the Blues* (New York: Stein and Day, 1970); and Bill C. Malone and Judith McCulloh, eds., *Stars of Country Music* (Urbana: University of Illinois Press, 1975).

2. For discographical information on the I.C. Glee Club and all other Memphis groups, see Appendix I.

3. This aspect of field recording in Memphis is covered in Kip Lornell, "The Field Recording of American Folk Music: A Case Study from Tennessee in 1928," *Tennessee Folklore Society Bulletin*, no. 4 (Winter 1981), pp. 153–59; reprinted in *The Sounds of People and Places: Read-*

ings in the Geography of American Folk and Popular Music, ed. George Carney (Washington, D.C.: University Press of America, 1987), pp. 91–101.

4. For further information see Colin Escott and Martin Hawkins, *Sun Records: The Brief History of the Legendary Record Label* (New York: Quick Fox Press, 1980).

5. Robert Reed, interviewed by Doug Seroff in Memphis, Tennessee, June 1979; transcript in the author's possession.

6. Cedrick Hayes and Robert Laughton, "Postwar Gospel Records," typescript.

7. Earl Malone, interviewed by Kip Lornell in Memphis, Tennessee, October 11, 1980. Unless indicated otherwise, all interviews were conducted by the author in Memphis; tape and transcript copies are deposited in the Mississippi Valley Collection, Brister Library, Memphis State University.

8. Jethroe Bledsoe, interview, May 21, 1982.

9. Rounder Records, *The Atomic Cafe,* 1982.

10. Earl Malone, interviewed by Doug Seroff in Memphis, Tennessee, August 5, 1979; transcript in the author's possession.

11. Grover Blake, interview, July 10, 1982.

12. Ernest Moore, interview, May 21, 1982.

13. Jack Franklin, interview, May 21, 1982.

14. Ibid.

15. Malone interview, August 5, 1979.

16. Eugene Walton, interview, February 2, 1982.

17. David Clark, interviewed by Kip Lornell in Jackson, Mississippi, February 25, 1982.

18. Ibid.

19. Ibid.

20. Roger Meeden and George Moonoogian, "Duke Records—The Early Years, An Interview with David J. Mattis," *Whiskey, Women, and . . . ,* no. 1 (June 1984), p. 18.

21. Ibid., pp. 18–26.

22. Style Wooten, interview, July 17, 1982.

23. Flozell Leland, interview, June 14, 1982.

24. Huddie Moore, interview, February 2, 1983.

25. *Memphis Press-Scimitar,* February 1, 1929, p. 20.

26. Personal correspondence, Robert W. O'Brien to Kip Lornell, July 27, 1982.

27. Eugene Walton, interview, March 14, 1981.

28. Ibid., February 5, 1983.

29. Ibid., March 14, 1981.

30. Doug Seroff, liner notes, *"Bless My Bones": Memphis Gospel Radio—The 1950s,* Pea-Vine PLP 9051 (Tokyo, 1981).

31. Ibid., p. 1.

32. Ford Nelson, interview, June 2, 1982.

33. Nina Jai Daugherty, interview, May 21, 1981.

34. Nelson interview.

35. Ibid.

36. James Darling, interview, August 2, 1983.

37. Seroff, *"Bless My Bones,"* p. 2.

38. Ibid. The record contains transcriptions by the Southern Wonders, the Sunset Travelers, the Dixie Nightingales, the Brewsteraires, and the Spirit of Memphis.

"Blessed Are the Dead"

Black religious quartet singing has been a significant part of American folk and popular music since at least the turn of the twentieth century. This book examines quartet singing in Memphis, Tennessee, over a sixty-year period during which nationally recognized groups like the Spirit of Memphis and locally influential artists like the Middle Baptist Quartet, the Harps of Melody, and the Gospel Writers helped to create a unique musical culture. The continuous interaction between folk and popular culture that has characterized Afro-American quartet singing since Reconstruction is one of the recurring themes in this book. Between 1945 and 1955 black American gospel quartets became a highly visible and influential part of popular musical culture. Such peaks, which also occurred less dramatically during the 1920s, resulted when quartet singing was "discovered" by the printed and electronic agents of popular culture.

Similar cycles of popularity mark the history of many types of Afro-American vernacular music. Another example can be found in jazz, when the big "swing" bands of the late 1930s and early 1940s made millions aware of the genius of Duke Ellington, Cab Calloway, Count Basie, and Jimmie Lunceford. Jazz took another, albeit smaller, leap into general popularity in the late 1950s, propelled by artists such as Dave Brubeck, Thelonius Monk, and Miles Davis. The "blues revival" of the 1960s brought the music of Robert

Johnson, Skip James, Muddy Waters, B. B. King, John Hurt, and Gary Davis into homes across the country. A more striking example is the early 1970s ragtime revival when the movie *The Sting* focused widespread attention on this long-moribund musical genre. Yet the popularization of these genres simply could not be sustained. The very nature of popular culture is ephemeral, as exemplified by the boogie-woogie fad of the late 1930s when Pete Johnson, Meade Lux Lewis, and Albert Ammons were accepted by a large audience. Just as a small, loyal audience for boogie-woogie still exists, black gospel quartets have retained a following in their community.

Black American quartet singing has also been characterized by the tension between secular and sacred ambitions. This theme recurs throughout its history as groups and individuals have debated whether to stay with God or join the world of popular music. As far back as the turn of the century, groups such as the Dinwiddie Colored Quartet were abandoning their sacred roots for pop music careers. And as the stakes grew larger, the temptations increased. During the 1940s college groups such as the Hampton Institute Quartet and church groups such as the Golden Gate Quartet turned to secular music and gained an even greater multiracial audience. The more conservative church members objected to this trend and tended to ostracize those who favored "worldly" gain over spiritual wealth. (This secular-sacred phenomenon is not limited to quartets. Aretha Franklin and "Little" Richard Penniman, for instance, have moved back and forth between these two worlds; and gospel quartets have supplied more than their share of great singers, like Sam Cooke and Lou Rawls, to secular music.)

The support of a white audience is also noteworthy in the development of religious quartet singing. The Fisk Jubilee Singers prospered partly because of the interest shown in them by multiracial supporters in the United States but also around the world. Other institutional quartets in later years were careful to go after the money found in the pockets of white listeners and record company executives. Following World War II, the Golden Gate Quartet's movement into Café Society and their eventual expatriation underscores the importance they placed on pleasing white audiences. Anglo-American interest in quartets has taken an upward turn in recent years, though not in terms of popular support for the music. The fact is that nearly all of the historical and discographical research related to black American gospel quartets has been done by whites, a trend with parallels in other fields of Afro-American music such as blues and jazz.

"Happy in the Service of the Lord" brings to light three points specifically related to quartet singing in Memphis. First, the fact that at least eighty black gospel quartets were active in Memphis clearly demonstrates the importance of this style as an expression of religious music. Second, Memphis has been a center for quartet singing in the Mid-South and, arguably, the entire country. The number of local semiprofessional and professional quartets, the frequent programs held in the Mason's Temple, and the importance of performances by Memphis's community quartets outside of the city, all support this point. Finally, the quartet tradition in Memphis is not extinct. The a cappella groups that sing in local churches still retain a traditional repertoire and performance style, while the popularity of more modern quartets like the Spirit of Memphis indicates that quartets will be part of the city's religious music for many years to come.

Quartet singing is not Memphis's only form of black religious musical expression. The music of Pentecostal or "holiness" worshipers, for example, is also quite strong. The headquarters for one of the largest black Pentecostal sects, the Church of God in Christ, is located in Memphis. The works of important black gospel composers such as Thomas A. Dorsey and Rev. Charles Tindley, which are often performed by choral groups or choirs, have also been important in the local Baptist and Methodist churches since the 1930s. Such religious traditions and other secular musical styles such as blues are related in different ways to the Memphis quartet tradition. But each has forged its own unique heritage that demands separate, book-length treatment. To include these and other types of black religious music in this book would have obscured my tight focus on quartets.

Let me suggest some other unexplored avenues for research in local religious music. Along with the musical traditions of the Church of God in Christ, Memphis has bred two nationally recognized gospel composers, Lucie E. Campbell and Rev. W. Herbert

The Sons of Jehovah, circa 1962, were a premier "hard gospel" quartet in Memphis, beginning in about 1955: Fred Newsome, Frank Perkins, Arthur Saunders, Frank Black. *Author's collection.*

Formed about 1930, the Royal Harmony Four was still active in 1980: James Randolph, Jr., Eddie Crawford, Tony Bobbins, John Friday, Jack Miller. *Author's collection.*

The Evening Doves continued a capella harmony singing into the middle 1960s: (*top*) Florence Wiley, Mary Alice (?), Louise Pegues, Mary Jones, Marie Walton; (*bottom*) Floyd Wiley. *Courtesy of Marie Walton.*

The Brewsteraires sang together for nearly twenty-five years before breaking up in the early 1970s. *Author's collection.*

In August 1983 the Harps of Melody sang at the Gospel Quartet Heritage Program: Clara Anderson, Mabel Robinson, Hazel Young, Elizabeth Morris. *Photo by Lynn Abbott.*

The Pattersonaires performing at the August 1983 Gospel Quartet Heritage Program: Willie Neal, Jimmie Mountain, Ernest Donaldson, Roy Neal, Alphonzo Davis, James Shelton. *Photo by Lynn Abbott.*

The Spirit of Memphis on stage at the Gospel Quartet Heritage Program, August 1983: Melvin Mosley, Robert Reed, James Darling, Earl Malone. *Photo by Lynn Abbott.*

James Darling, August 1983. *Photograph by Lynn Abbott.*

Jack Steptoe & Melvin Mosley (*standing*) rehearse with Robert Reed, Earl Malone, and James Darling prior to the August 1983 Gospel Quartet Heritage Program. *Photo by Lynn Abbott.*

Brewster. The Smithsonian Institution conducted symposia on both Campbell (1983) and Brewster (1982), but these discussions by no means exhausted their subjects. Also, the influence of black gospel music in Memphis on the local soul, rockabilly, and blues tradition should be examined. Elvis Presley, among others, listened to black gospel music while growing up in Memphis. A critical exploration of this interaction would be a valuable addition to our knowledge of American popular music.

Outside of Memphis there are numerous research topics. Basic information regarding the Fisk Jubilee Singers and the Hampton University groups lies buried in poorly financed, underorganized archives—which is probably the fate of much information on other institutionally affiliated quartets. But the jubilee singing movement must be studied for it is fundamental to an understanding of quartet history; moreover, it is of critical importance to our general understanding of black American cultural, economic, social, and musical history.

Although much of the quartet research has focused on groups that made commercial recordings, the recorded groups in cities like Chicago, St. Louis, and Baltimore basically remain enigmas. The same is true for entire states such as South Carolina and Kentucky. Intensive local histories or statewide surveys are vital not only for their musical information but also for their cultural implications. A modular, interdisciplinary approach to the study of black culture and music is needed because the two offer a microcosm that can readily be fit into a larger picture.

Perhaps the most pressing concern is the decided lack of research on community quartets, which are the backbone of the gospel quartet tradition. Such groups are the least glamorous to research—most of them did not make commercial recordings, never traveled extensively, nor had a nationwide following. However, community quartets have had a strong local and regional impact, tend to reflect regional styles of singing, and are the wellspring for nearly all of the commercially successful groups.

Unfortunately these research topics are not often promoted in our universities due to their interdisciplinary nature. Such musical communities are usually below the scrutiny of most historians, while sociologists generally do not document musical activity. The worst offenders are most music departments, which woefully neglect or totally ignore American music, or else relegate it to second- or third-class status. No literature or history curricula in the United States downplay indigenous topics to the same degree as do departments of music. This pejorative observation applies to *all* types of American music, not just vernacular black religious music.

The present study underscores the interdisciplinary path that music research can take. Scholars may wish to pay closer attention to the spatial aspects of music. It is undeniable that perspectives from cultural geography can be rewarding and exciting because they present a discipline sadly overlooked by students of American music. Studies of black gospel music should closely examine the unique communities from which these styles spring. The importance of performance practices and community studies serves to reinforce the role that anthropology can play in any examination of music.

The narrow research focus on historical and discographical matters makes it impossible, in this book, to offer cross-regional comparisons. From a cultural point of view, for example, how do the roles taken by Memphis quartet trainers relate to those in other cities? Is quartet training always a male domain? What of the written bylaws utilized by some Memphis groups? Do quartets across the country adhere to the same standards or do they even formalize such rules?

Geographical research, which included plotting the performance migration patterns of the Spirit of Memphis, raised questions regarding the routes taken by other groups. Was the Spirit of Memphis's travel pattern unusual or did the group follow the same patterns as other professional quartets? Furthermore, how do social networks influence performance travel patterns in other sections of the country? These and many other tantalizing questions await future researchers.

Another area of serious concern for scholars in American music is the marked dearth of published discographies. In black religious music, for instance, there is no comprehensive listing. *Blues and Gospel Records 1902–1943* is the most authoritative, but it neglects important groups like the Fisk University Quartet and covers only a specific time period. There is *no* published listing available for the years following World War II, which is a terrible handicap because of the importance of the record industry in disseminating repertoire, vocal techniques, and other related matters. The compilation of such a discography is a difficult task; however, the accomplishment of this and the other research areas that I have outlined would represent a significant step forward in our comprehensive understanding of black American music.

Memphis Quartet Listing

This is an exhaustive list of Afro-American gospel quartets active in Memphis between the mid-1920s and 1987. The groups are divided into three categories—professional, semiprofessional, and community—according to their status. A few groups like the Southern Wonders are found in more than one category because their status changed over the years. The approximate dates each group was active as a harmony quartet are given in parentheses. Several groups—the Gableaires, the Jubilee Hummingbirds, and the Southern Jubilees—are still active but now perform more modern gospel music.

Professional
Southern Wonders (1952–57)
Spirit of Memphis (1950–62)
Sunset Travelers (1953–60)

Semiprofessional
Dixie Nightingales (1952–62)
Gableaires (1955–61)
Jones Brothers Quartet
  (1954–64)
Jordan Wonders (1953–60)
Jubilee Hummingbirds
  (1954–62)
Sons of Jehovah (1953–63)
Spirit of Memphis (1945–50,
  1962–present)
Spiritual Travelers (1954–65)
Sunset Travelers (1960–present)

Community
Bells of Harmony (1948–54)
Brewsteraires (1947–72)
Busyline Soft Singers (1931–38)
Campbellaires (1947–59)
Conner Gee Singers (1938–47)
Delta Friendly Four of Memphis
  (1946–49)
Dixie Wonders (1954–63)
Drifting Clouds Quartet
  (1947–50)
E. and S. (Construction Company)
  Quartet (1932–36)
Evening Doves (1950–60)
Fitch Brothers Quartet
  (1942–48)
Friendly Echoes (1951–60)
Golden Echoes (1948–51)

Golden Stars (1939–47)
Gospel Tones (1948–52)
Gospel Travelers (1939–62)
Gospel Writer Junior Boys
(1947–52)
Gospel Writer Junior Girls
(1939–49)
Gospel Writers (1937–55,
1976–present)
Harmonious Spirituals (1941–45)
Harmonizers (1976–present)
Harmony Four (1927–32)
Harps of Melody (1950–present)
Hiawatha Glee Club (1931–35)
Hollywood Specials (1930–40)
Holy Ghost Spirituals
(1976–present)
I.C. Glee Club (1927–38)
I.C. Harmony Boys (1932–39)
I.C. Hummingbirds (1934–41)
I.C. Quartet #2 (1930–40)
Independent Quartet (1932–46)
Jollyaires (1947–52)
Keystone Masters of Harmony
(1947–53)
L. C. and I. Singers (1952–56)
Lake Grove Quartet (1941–48)
Loving Junior Girls (1942–46)
M. and N. Junior Girls (1939–43)
M. and N. Singers (1937–48)
Majestic Soft Singers (1945–55)
Memphis Spiritual Four
(1936–70)
Middle Baptist Quartet
(1933–40)
Missouri-Pacific Lines Booster
Quartet (1927–35)
Mount Olive Wonders (1927–33)
Mount Pisgah Glee Singers
(1941–52)
National Christian Singers
(1941–51)

New Gospel Writers
(1986–present)
Old Red Rose Quartet (1925–30)
Orange Mound Harmonizers
(1932–35)
Orange Mound Specials
(1934–39)
Pattersonaires (1953–64)
Rock Island Quartet (1941–50)
Royal Harmony Four
(1931–present)
S. and W. (Construction Com-
pany) Quartet (1928–30)
Songbirds of the South
(1948–56)
Southern Bells (1947–53)
Southern Harmony Boys
(1937–45)
Southern Jubilees (1945–65)
Southern Wonders (1941–52)
Spirit of Memphis Junior Quartette
(1933–39)
Spirit of Memphis Quartette
(1930–45)
Spiritual Pilgrims (1943–68)
Sunshine Jolly Boosters Club
Quartet (1941–54)
T. M. and S. Quartet (1927–30)
True Friends Gospel Singers
(1939–50)
Union Soft Singers (1938–46)
United Specials (1975–present)
Vance Ensemble (1974–present)
Veteran Jubilees (1952–59)
Walker Specials (1951–55)
Wells Spirituals (1949–60)
Willing Four Soft Singers
(1946–present)
Zion Glee Singers (1938–42)
Zion Hill Spirituals (1937–78)

II

Jethroe Bledsoe's 1952 Travel Diary for the Spirit of Memphis

April 3—Hutchison, Kansas
April 6—Davenport, Iowa
April 7—Omaha, Nebraska
April 8—Des Moines, Iowa
April 10—Youngstown, Ohio
April 11—Cleveland, Ohio
April 13—Newark, New Jersey, and Philadelphia, Pennsylvania
April 14—Pittsburgh, Pennsylvania
April 17—Humbolt, Tennessee
April 20—Atlanta, Georgia
April 21—Memphis, Tennessee
April 22—Memphis, Tennessee
April 23—Memphis, Tennessee
April 24—Memphis, Tennessee
April 25—Oxford, Mississippi
April 27—Memphis, Tennessee

May 4—Austin, Texas
May 18—El Dorado, Arkansas
May 19—Gladwater, Texas
May 21—Shreveport, Louisiana
May 22—Wichita Falls, Texas
May 23—Sherman, Texas
May 26—San Antonio, Texas
May 28—Tyler, Texas

May 29—Greenville, Texas
May 30—Dallas, Texas

June 6—Fort Worth, Texas
June 9—Monroe City, Texas
June 13—Pensacola, Florida
June 14—Birmingham, Alabama
June 15—Birmingham, Alabama
June 16—Montgomery, Alabama
June 20—Memphis, Tennessee
June 21—Oxford, Mississippi
June 22—Durham, North Carolina
June 23—Durham, North Carolina
June 24—Durham, North Carolina
June 25—Durham, North Carolina
June 29—Oxford, Mississippi

July 1—Washington, D.C.
July 6—Buffalo, New York
July 7—Buffalo, New York
July 8—Buffalo, New York
July 11—Cincinnati, Ohio
July 13—Detroit, Michigan
July 14—Detroit, Michigan
July 15—Detroit, Michigan
July 16—Detroit, Michigan

July 18—Dayton, Ohio
July 19—Welch, West Virginia
July 20—Beckley, West Virginia,
   and Charleston, West Virginia
July 22—Lambert, Mississippi
July 27—New Orleans, Louisiana
July 28—Mobile, Alabama

August 1—Memphis, Tennessee
August 3—Topeka, Kansas
August 4—Topeka, Kansas
August 6—El Paso, Texas
August 7—Tucson, Arizona
August 8—Phoenix, Arizona
August 10—Oakland, California
August 11—San Francisco,
   California
August 12—Los Angeles,
   California
August 22—Pine Bluff, Arkansas
August 24—Houston, Texas

August 28—Lambert, Mississippi
August 31—Memphis, Tennessee

September 8—Albany, Georgia
September 14—New Orleans,
   Louisiana
September 15—Baton Rouge,
   Louisiana
September 16—Gladstone, Texas
September 17—Newton, Texas
September 19—San Antonio,
   Texas
September 21—Mexa, Texas
September 22—Longview, Texas
September 24—Stanton,
   Oklahoma
September 25—Tulsa, Oklahoma
September 28—Topeka, Kansas
September 30—Arlington,
   Tennessee

Memphis Gospel Quartet
Discography

This is a comprehensive listing of the commercial and noncommercial recordings by Memphis gospel quartets between 1928 and 1987. The serious gaps found in this discography fall between 1960 and 1980 when several Memphis quartets were recorded by local companies whose files are nonexistent. The High Water Record files include so many unissued songs that for clarity's sake only that label's issued performances are listed. The selections designated "Perkins Disc" are home recordings done by Frank Perkins, founder of the Sons of Jehovah. The format for this discography is adapted from Godrich and Dixon, *Blues and Gospel Records 1902–1943.* Long-playing reissues of older material are also included because many of the original 78-rpm and 45-rpm issues are very difficult to locate. Reissues are italicized to differentiate them from their original issue.

Brewsteraires

Odell Rice (baritone), Nathaniel Peck (tenor and lead-1), Henry Reed (bass), Solomon Alston (tenor and lead)
Memphis, Tennessee, December 26, 1951

F-1008	Where Shall I Be When That First Trumpet Sounds	Chess 1502 and *Sunbox 105*
F-1009	(The Lord Gave Me) Wings for My Soul	Chess 1502 and *Sunbox 105*
	(I Heard a Voice) in the Middle of the Night	Chess unissued

Memphis, Tennessee, circa 1953

Hold On	Dot 1132
That's Enough (1)	Dot 1132

| Jasper Walls | Dot 1133 |
| More of Jesus, Less of Me | Dot 1133 |

Memphis, Tennessee, circa 1953
Add D. K. Rodgers (baritone and lead-2)

| King's Highway (1 and 2) | Pea-Vine PLP 9051 |

Add Melvin Lee (guitar)

| Wait until My Change Comes | Pea-Vine PLP 9051 |

Memphis, Tennessee, 1972
James Irby (lead) replaces Henry Reed; add Jimmy Bessler (piano) and (?) Bogart (electric bass)

| Book of the Seven Seals, Part 1 | Private pressing |
| Book of the Seven Seals, Part 2 | Private pressing |

Dixie Nightingales

Ollie Hoskins (lead), Willie Neal (baritone), Roy Neal (tenor), Willie Davis (bass), Willie Horner (guitar), unknown piano
Memphis, Tennessee, circa 1958

| I've Been Lifted | Pepper 910 |
| I've Got a New Home | Pepper 910 |

Memphis, Tennessee, circa 1958

| In My Saviour's Care | Pea-Vine PLP 9051 |

Nashville, Tennessee, circa 1961

My Destiny	Nashboro 728
Now I Lay Me Down to Sleep	Nashboro 728
I Would Not Be a Sinner	Nashboro 764
I'll Go with You	Nashboro 764

Nashville, Tennessee, circa 1962

| Pleading for Me | Nashboro 808 |
| Death Is Riding | Nashboro 808 |

Gospel Tones

Jack Stepter (lead), G. T. Widdington (lead), Tim Allen (baritone), C. D. Davidson (tenor), Cicero Lewis (bass)
Memphis, Tennessee, December 10, 1951

Noah	Sun unissued
Get Away Jordan	Sun unissued
Rock My Soul	Sun unissued
Motherless Children	Sun unissued
Lord Be Near Me—Hear Me	Sun unissued

Gospel Travelers

John Spencer (baritone), Troy Yarborough (bass), Ray Hurley (tenor and guitar), Eugene Walton (tenor and lead)

Memphis, Tennessee, Spring 1952

	God's Chariot, Part 1	Duke G-1 and *Krazy Kat* 7424
	God's Chariot, Part 2	Duke G-1 and *Krazy Kat* 7424

Houston, Texas, Summer 1952

An unknown number of unissued titles for Duke Records

Memphis, Tennessee, circa 1953

An unknown number of unissued titles for Modern Records

Memphis, Tennessee, circa 1955

TR-21	Man at the Door	Chariot 30
TR-22	Praying Time	Chariot 30

Gospel Trumpets

Unknown male singers

Memphis, Tennessee, circa 1957

Stop by Here	Perkins Disc
Let Jesus Lead You All the Way	Perkins Disc
Troubled 'bout My Soul	Perkins Disc

Gospel Writers

George Rooks (tenor and lead-1), David Ward (fifth), Willie Wilson (tenor and lead-2), Jesse Allen (bass), Jimmy Allen (baritone and lead-3)

Memphis, Tennessee, June 28, 1982

Oh, My Lordy Lord (2 and 3)	High Water 420

Memphis, Tennessee, October 29, 1982

Blind Barnabas (1)	High Water 420

Memphis, Tennessee, February 24, 1983

Kevin Lott replaces Jimmy Allen

New Born Soul (1)	High Water 1002

Memphis, Tennessee, May 23, 1983

Roy Neal replaces David Ward; George Rooks dropped

Gospel Writer Boys Are We (2)	High Water 1002

Up above My Head I Hear Music in the   High Water
  Air (2)   1002

Harmonizers

Elijah Ruffin (bass and lead-1), McClendon Cox (tenor and lead-2),
Julius Guy (baritone), Hershell McDonald (tenor and lead-3)
Memphis, Tennessee, June 14, 1982
    I'll Be Satisfied (1)   High Water 419
Memphis, Tennessee, June 28, 1982
    Trampin' (3)   High Water 419
Memphis, Tennessee, February 17, 1983
    Roll, Jordan, Roll (3)   High Water
                                                         1002

Memphis, Tennessee, February 24, 1983
    My Lord Is Writing (1)   High Water
                                                         1002

    I'm Leaning on the Everlasting Arm   High Water
      (1 and 2)   1002

Harps of Melody

Clara Anderson (tenor and lead), Mabel Robinson (tenor), Hazel Young
(baritone), Elizabeth Morris (bass), unknown instruments
Memphis, Tennessee, circa 1968
012   Lord Bless the Weary Soldier in Vietnam   Philwood G-207
013   King Jesus Will Roll All My Burdens Away   Philwood G-207
Memphis, Tennessee, February 17, 1983
Joe Dysen replaces Hazel Young; instruments dropped
      I'm Going to Sing and Make Melody unto   High Water
        the Lord   1002
Memphis, Tennessee, May 2, 1983
Hazel Young replaces Joe Dysen
      Blind Bartimus   High Water
                                                     1002

Holy Ghost Spirituals

Gladys West (baritone and lead-1), Sylvia Smith (alto and lead-2),
Juanita Wilson (baritone and lead-3), Armeta Nixon (tenor), Lorine
Henry (tenor)
Memphis, Tennessee, May 3, 1983
Armeta Nixon dropped
      Old Landmark (3)   High Water
                                                     1002

Lorine Henry dropped
      Ninety-nine and a Half (2)   High Water
                                                     1002

Talk to the Man Upstairs (1)   High Water
                                                       1002

I.C. Colored Glee Club

C. H. Evans (first tenor), R. S. Saunders (second tenor), E. L. Rhodes
(baritone), L. S. Brown (bass)
Memphis, Tennessee, February 16, 1928

400252-B	Don't You Hear the Bells A-Ringing	OKeh unissued
400253-B	If I Get Inside	OKeh unissued
400254-B	Four and Twenty Elders on Their Knees	OKeh unissued
400255-B	God Told the Widow to Cook All She Had	OKeh unissued

Atlanta, Georgia, March 18, 1929
I.C. Glee Quartet, presumably the same personnel

402347-B	So Glad Trouble Don't Last Always	OKeh 8681
402348-B	He Pardoned Me	OKeh 8726
402349-B	Come On, Don't You Want to Go	OKeh 8726
402350-B	I'm Going Home on the Chickasaw Train	OKeh 8710
402351-B	God Told the Poor Widow to Cook All She Had	OKeh 8710
402352-A	When They Ring Dem Golden Bells	OKeh 8681

New York City, October 23, 1930
Unknown piano (a)

404495-B	Riding on the Seminole	OKeh 8929
404496-A	All My Sins Taken Away	OKeh 8837
404497-B	Panama to Chi	OKeh 8929
404498-B	When the Leaves Turn Red and Fall	OKeh 8848
404499-B	Church Meeting	OKeh unissued
404500-C	Gambler, You Can't Ride This Train	OKeh 8848
404501-B	Sermon Revelation Fifth Chapter	OKeh unissued
404502-A	I Shall Not Be Removed (a)	OKeh 8872

New York City, October 24, 1930

| 404503-B | If I Could Hear My Mother Pray Again | OKeh 8837 |
| 404504-B | Lord Have Mercy When I Come to Die | OKeh 8872 |

Pattersonaires

Ernest Donaldson (baritone and lead-1), Roy Neal (tenor and lead-2),
Willie Neal (tenor and lead-3), James Shelton (lead-4), Willie Gordon
(piano and lead-5).
Memphis, Tennessee, circa 1966
         Four titles for the Chalice Record Company
Memphis, Tennessee, May 23, 1983
         He's Worthy (4)   High Water
                                                       1002

Why Not Try My God? (3 and 4)	High Water 1002

Memphis, Tennessee, November 6, 1983
Derrick Jackson (organ on all tracks), Aubrey Williams (bass guitar on all tracks except side 2, track 1), Squire Marshall (bass guitar on side 2, track 1), Alphonzo Davis (background and lead-6), Jimmie Mountain (tenor-7), William Fletcher (drums on all tracks)

I Shall See Him Face to Face (6)	High Water 1004
Old Landmark (2)	High Water 1004

Memphis, Tennessee, January 8, 1984

Call Me (Here I Am) (4 and 7)	High Water 1004
Book of the Seven Seals (1, 5, 6, and 7)	High Water 1004

Memphis, Tennessee, January 17, 1984

I Waited for an Answer (4 and 7)	High Water 1004
I Feel Something Drawing and Pulling Me (4)	High Water 1004
How Great Thou Art (4)	High Water 1004
I'm His, He's Mine (3 and 7)	High Water 1004

Memphis, Tennessee, March 19, 1984

Faith Moves Mountains (2, 4, and 6)	High Water 1004

Silvertones

Unknown male quartet
Memphis, Tennessee, April 2, 1950

Beautiful City	Perkins Disc
Something within Me	Perkins Disc

Memphis, Tennessee, circa 1952–54

Good Morning to Heaven	Perkins Disc
My Life Is in God's Hands	Perkins Disc
Something within Me	Perkins Disc
Beautiful City	Perkins Disc
Shadrack	Perkins Disc

Songbirds of the South

Mary Reddick (lead-1), Cassietta Baker (lead-2), Evelyn Broadnax (tenor), Ernestine Whitehead (tenor), Elizabeth Darling (bass and piano-3)

Memphis, Tennessee, June 20, 1953
  Jesus Met the Woman at the Well (1 and 2) Pea-Vine PLP
                      9051

Memphis, Tennessee, July 24, 1953
  99½ Won't Do (2)   Pea-Vine PLP
                      9051
  Where Could I Go? (2 and 3)   Pea-Vine PLP
                      9051

Sons of Jehovah

Frank Perkins (vocals), others unknown
Memphis, Tennessee, April 10, 1952
  Rock My Soul   Perkins Disc
Memphis, Tennessee, March 28, 1956
  WDIA Saturday Song   Perkins Disc
  Teach Me (Our Prayer)   Perkins Disc
Memphis, Tennessee, April 5, 1957
Add unknown guitar and Brother Rodgers (lead)
  He Will Understand   Perkins Disc
  You Must be Born   Perkins Disc
Memphis, Tennessee, circa 1950–58
Unknown instruments and vocalists
  If Jesus Holds My Hand, I Believe Perkins Disc
  I'll Go   Perkins Disc
  Go and Tell the Reds We're Gonna Win Perkins Disc
Unknown drums and guitar
  On Calvary   Perkins Disc
  John the Revelator   Perkins Disc
Unknown guitar
  I'm Waiting and Watching   Perkins Disc
  On an Island   Perkins Disc
  What Could I Do?   Perkins Disc
  Something Within   Perkins Disc
  I John Saw   Perkins Disc
Unknown drums and guitar
  WDIA, Part 2   Perkins Disc
Nashville, Tennessee, 1957–60
Frank Perkins (lead-1), Melvin Rodgers (lead-2), Willie Harrison (bass),
Aubrey Lee Smith (baritone), Jessie Macklin (tenor), William Ferris
(guitar), unknown piano, bass, and drums on most tracks
  High Cost of Living (1)   Nashboro 610
  Teach Me Jesus (2)   Nashboro 610
  Keep and Teach Me (1 and 2)   Nashboro 626
  The Holy Bible (1)   Nashboro 626

Waiting for Me (1)	Nashboro 645
Jesus Hear My Plea (2)	Nashboro 645
It's Me Lord (2)	Nashboro 669
We Are Blessed (1)	Nashboro 669
A Servant of God (1)	Nashboro 709
Let My People Go (1)	Nashboro 709
Gonna Travel On (1)	Nashboro 737
Our Troubles of Today (1)	Nashboro 737
Judgement Day Is Coming (1)	Nashboro 763
You Gotta Live Right (1)	Nashboro 763
The Story of Noah (1)	Nashboro 792
Left All Alone (1)	Nashboro 792
Pleading for God (1)	Nashboro 817
Story of the Hebrew Children (1)	Nashboro 817

Southern Jubilees

Don Taylor (tenor), Eugene Frazier (bass and lead-1), Lavone Smith
(tenor and lead-2), Calvin Mitchell (baritone), Jake MacIntosh (lead-3)
Memphis, Tennessee, December 19, 1951

There Is a Man in Jerusalem (1)	*Sunbox 105*
Forgive Me Lord (2)	*Sunbox 105*
He Never Left Me Alone (3)	*Sunbox 105*
Blessed Be Thy Name	Sun unissued

Southern Wonders

Rev. Ernest McKinney (lead-1), R. L. Weaver (lead-2), Artis Yancey
(bass), Ernest Moore (baritone), James Darling (lead-3), Henry Jack
Franklin (tenor), L. T. Blair (guitar), unknown drums (a)
Houston, Texas, circa 1952

ACA2170 How Much More Can I Bear? (1)	Peacock 1725
ACA2171 Come on over Here (2)	Peacock 1702
ACA2172 Gambling Man (1 and a)	Peacock 1711
ACA2173 Who Is That Knocking? (1 and 2)	Peacock 1702
ACA2174 There Is No Rest for the Weary (1, 3, and a)	Peacock 1711
ACA2175 Jesus Died for You and Me	Peacock unissued
ACA2452 I'll Fly Away (1 and 2)	Peacock 1725

Houston, Texas, circa 1953

ACA3164 My Jesus Is All (1, 2, and a)	Peacock 1750
ACA3165 I Was a Sinner (2)	Peacock 1750
ACA3217 The Chapel (2)	Peacock 1751
ACA3218 As an Eagle Stirreth Her Nest (1, 2, and a)	Peacock 1751

Memphis, Tennessee, February 17, 1953

Thank You, Jesus (1 and 2)	Pea-Vine PLP 9051

	More Like Jesus	WDIA Test

Memphis, Tennessee, September 1, 1953

	Anyhow	WDIA Test
	Lord Stand by Me (1 and 2)	Pea-Vine PLP 9051

Spirit of Memphis Quartet

(Memphis Gospel Singers) Jethroe Bledsoe (lead-1), Silas Steele (lead-2) Earl Malone (bass and lead-3), James Darling (baritone) Birmingham, Alabama, circa May 1949

	Happy in the Service of the Lord (1)	Hallelujah Spiritual
	How Many Times (1)	Hallelujah Spiritual
874	I'm Happy in the Service of the Lord (1)	De Luxe 3221 and *Pea-Vine PLP 9051*
875	My Life Is in His Hands (2)	De Luxe 3221

Cincinnati, Ohio, December 12, 1949
Wilbur Broadnax (lead-4)

K5812-2	On the Battlefield (1)	King 4358 and *King K-5020X*
K4513	Days Passed and Gone (1 and 2)	King 4340 and *King K-5020X*
K4514-3	He Never Left Me Alone (2)	King 4371 and King K-5020X
K5815	Blessed Are the Dead (1)	King 4340
K5816	If Jesus Had to Pray (2 and 4)	King 4371 and *King K-5020X*
K5817-2	Jesus, Jesus (2 and 4)	King 4358

Cincinnati, Ohio, April 1950

K5899-2	I'll Never Forget (1 and 4)	King 4407
K5900-1	Calvary (2 and 4)	King 4392 and *King K-5020X*
K5901-2	How Far I Am from Canaan (1 and 4)	King 4407
K5902-1	Make More Room for Jesus (1 and 4)	King 4392

Cincinnati, Ohio, December 9, 1950
James Keele replaces Earl Malone

K5995-2	Automobile to Glory (1 and 2)	King 4429
K5996	If You Make a Start to Heaven (1, 2, and 4)	King 4440

K5997   God's Got His Eye on You (1 and 2)   King 4440 and
                                                      King
                                                      K-5020X

K5998-2 I'll Go   King 4429 and
                                                      King
                                                      K-5020X

Cincinnati, Ohio, May 5, 1951
Earl Malone replaces James Keele; unknown organ (a)
K9041-1 Every Day and Every Hour (1 and 4)   King 4463
K9042   Everytime I Feel the Spirit (1, 2, and 4)   King 4471
K9043-1 World Prayer (1, 2, and a)   King 4463
K9044   Sign of Judgement (2)   King 4471 and
                                                      King
                                                      K-5020X

Cincinnati, Ohio, August 14, 1951
Unknown organ and piano (b)
K9074-1 That Awful Day (1 and 2)   King 4538 and
                                                      King
                                                      K-5020X

K9075   Tell Heaven I'm Coming (1 and 3)   King 4500 and
                                                      King
                                                      K-5020X

K9076-1 Ease My Troubled Mind (1 and 2)   King 4538 and
                                                      King
                                                      K-5020X

K9077   He Never Let Go My Hand (1 and 4)   King 4521 and
                                                      King
                                                      K-5020X

K9078   The Ten Commandments (1, 2, and b)   King 4500
K9079   The Atomic Telephone (1 and 2)   King 4521
Cincinnati, Ohio, August 10, 1952
Fred Howard replaces James Darling
K9160   Toll the Bell Easy (1 and 2)   King 4575 and
                                                      King
                                                      K-5020X

K9161   Jesus Brought Me Here (1 and 2)   King 4562 and
                                                      King
                                                      K-5020X

K9162-1 There's No Sorrow (1)   King 4614
K9163-1 Workin' till the Day Is Done (1)   King 4614 and
                                                      King
                                                      K-5020X

K9164   God's Amazing Grace (1 and 2)   King 4575

K9165	Just to Behold His Face	King 4562 and *King K-5020X*

Memphis, Tennessee, October 7, 1952

K9179-1	Lord Jesus, Part 1 (1)	King 4576 and *Folklyric 9045*
K9180-1	Lord Jesus, Part 2 (1)	King 4576 and *Folklyric 9045*

The Spirit of Memphis's King recordings have been reissued many times on the following albums: Audio Lab EP 7, EP 8, EP 9, EP 19, and EP 20; King LP 573, LP 577, LP 942, and LP 954; Parlo PMD 1070 and PMD 1085; Polydor 657126; and Vogue V115, V116, V117, V120, V122, V124, and V149. It is so difficult to determine which issues are in print as of June 1987 that all of these issues are listed.

Houston, Texas, circa June 1953
Spirit of Memphis and unknown drums

ACA2374	God Save America (3 and 4)	Peacock 1710
ACA2375	Surely, Surely, Amen (1)	Peacock 1710
ACA2412	Since Jesus Came into My Heart (1)	Peacock 1717
ACA2413	I Will Trust in the Lord (1)	Peacock 1717
ACA2415	What Could I Do?	Peacock 1734

Houston, Texas, circa February 1954
Unknown trombone (c), piano and drums (d)

ACA2711	When Mother's Gone (1 and c)	Peacock 1730
ACA2756	I'll Tell It (2 and d)	Peacock 1754
ACA2757	He's a Friend of Mine (1, 4, and d)	Peacock 1730
ACA2758	Sweet Hour of Prayer (1 and a)	Peacock 1734

Memphis, Tennessee, circa 1954–55

Honey in the Rock	Perkins Disc
He Walks with Me	Perkins Disc
On Calvary	Perkins Disc
I'll Be Satisfied	Perkins Disc
Search Me, Lord	Perkins Disc

Houston, Texas, circa June 1955
Willie Jefferson (2) replaces Silas Steele and Wilbur Broadnax; L. T. Blair (guitar); unknown drums (e)

ACA3128	Home in the Sky (1 and a)	Peacock 1746
ACA3129	Standing by the Bedside (2, 3, and d)*	Peacock 1746
ACA3130	Sinner Make a Change (2 and e)	Peacock 1805
ACA3131	He'll Never Let Me Fall	Peacock 1754

*piano on this cut may be Napoleon Brown
Memphis, Tennessee, February 15, 1956
Joe Hinton (lead-5), Fred Howard (baritone and lead-6), Bobby Mack (lead-7)

	Two Little Fishes and Five Loaves of Bread (1 and 7)	WDIA Test
	Blessed Are the Poor in Spirit (1)	WDIA Test

Memphis, Tennessee, June 4, 1956

	Milky White Way (5 and 6)	Pea Vine PLP 9051
	The Lord Will Make a Way	WDIA Test

Memphis, Tennessee, late 1956

	Sending up Material	WDIA Test
	Walk of Life	WDIA Test
	I Don't Know Why	WDIA Test
	Savior, Don't Pass Me By	WDIA Test

Houston, Texas, late 1956

	I Found Something (1)	Peacock 1769
	If It Ain't One Thing (1 and 5)	Peacock 1769
	I Need Thee (5)	Peacock 1766

Houston, Texas, circa 1957–58
Bobby Mack (tenor and lead-7) replaces Fred Howard; Joe Johnson replaces L. T. Blair

FR2030	Lost in Sin (5)	Peacock 1766
FR2031	When (5)	Peacock 1779
FR2042	Story of Jesus (2)	Peacock 1779
FR2043	The Lord Loves Me (1 and 5)	Peacock 1785
FR2070	The Great Love (5)	Peacock 1785
FR2071	In the Garden (1)	Peacock 1798
FR2086	It Won't Be Long Now (1 and 3)	Peacock 1805
FR2087	Sinner Make a Change (see ACA3130)	Peacock 1805

Houston, Texas, circa 1959–60

FR8010	Doctor Jesus (1)	Peacock 1815
FR8011	'Twill be Glory (1)	Peacock 1815

Unknown drums added

	Further up the Road	Peacock 1828
	What Are You Doing in Your Town (1 and 5)	Peacock 1828
	If I Should Miss Heaven (1)	Peacock 1847
	Why? (3)	Peacock PLP109
	Storm of Life (1)	Peacock PLP109
	Take Your Burden to the Lord (1)	Peacock PLP109
	Somebody Here Lord (4 and 7)	Peacock PLP109
	Ease My Troubling Mind (7)	Peacock PLP109

Singing Won't Be in Vain (1)	Peacock PLP109
Walking with Jesus (1)	Peacock PLP109
Jesus Loves Me (1)	Peacock PLP109

Memphis, Tennessee, circa 1967

Pay Day (1 and 2)	Peacock 3096
My Explanation (1 and 2)	Peacock 3096

Houston, Texas, circa 1967

William Dixon replaces Joe Johnson; add Brown Berry (electric bass), unknown drummer, and William Walton (second lead-2)

My Old Home Town (1)	Peacock 3117
I'm in His Care (1 and 2)	Peacock 3117

Houston, Texas, circa 1968

In the Water (1)	Peacock 3150
Go Get Water (1)	Peacock 3150
Christian's Chain Gang (1 and 2)	Peacock 3173
Voo-doo-ism (1)	Peacock 3173

Memphis, Tennessee, December 8, 1971

Unknown personnel

See What the End Will Do	Home Boy
Swing Down	Home Boy

Memphis, Tennessee, circa early 1970s

Unknown personnel, but presumably with Joe Hinton on lead since the record is billed as Joe Hinton with the Spirit of Memphis

41158-A See What the End Will Be	Gospel Express
41158-B Swing Down	Gospel Express

Nashville, Tennessee, 1972

Fred Howard replaces Bobby Mack; all instruments dropped

40 Long Years	Randy's Spirituals-1025
Jesus Traveled	Randy's Spirituals-1025
Morning Train	Randy's Spirituals-1025
Talking about Jesus	Randy's Spirituals-1025
I'm a Pilgrim	Randy's Spirituals-1025

Swing Down (1)	Randy's Spirituals-1025
Woman at the Well	Randy's Spirituals-1025
You Better Run (1)	Randy's Spirituals-1025
Go Down Moses	Randy's Spirituals-1025

Memphis, Tennessee, circa 1975

You'd Better Run (1)	Gospel Train LP

Memphis, Tennessee, circa 1976
Unknown personnel, presumably similar to above

6-2276-A America	Gospel Express
6-2276-B Rest for the Weary	Gospel Express

Memphis, Tennessee, circa 1978
Percey Cole replaces Fred Howard (tenor); add Melvin Mosley (tenor and possibly lead on some selections) and Glenn Carr (drums)

Liar	ABEC ALP 7005
This Is a Mean Old World	ABEC ALP 7005
'Twill the Glory	ABEC ALP 7005
Lord, Count on Me	ABEC ALP 7005
See What the End Gonna Be	ABEC ALP 7005
My Friend	ABEC ALP 7005
I Thank You Lord	ABEC ALP 7005
Who Made the Pattern?	ABEC ALP 7005
There Is No God Like Thee	ABEC ALP 7005
Why?	ABEC ALP 7005

Memphis, Tennessee, May 3, 1983
Jimmie Allen replaces Fred Howard (lead-8); Jack Stepter replaces Earl Malone (lead-9); add Melvin Mosley (tenor and lead-10); Brown Berry dropped

Just to Behold His Face	High Water 1002

Hubert Crawford replaces William Dixon

Swing Down, Chariot (1)	High Water 1002

Memphis, Tennessee, March 16, 1984
Add Clifford Jackson (drums), Earl Malone, Hubert Crawford (lead-11 and bass guitar-f), and Brown Berry

I Believe in God (10 and f)	High Water 1005
Talking about a Child That Do Love Jesus (9)	High Water 1005
I John Saw (10)	High Water 1005

Memphis, Tennessee, March 21, 1984

We Are the Spirit of Memphis Quartet (10)	High Water 1005
Only Jesus (11)	High Water 1005
Jesus Traveled (3, 10, and f)	High Water 1005
Go, Get the Water (8)	High Water 1005
Singing Won't Be in Vain (10)	High Water 1005
Walking with Jesus (10)	High Water 1005

Memphis, Tennessee, July 2, 1984

Two Little Fishes and Five Loaves of Bread (10)	High Water 1005
The Lord Loves Me (11)	High Water 1005
If It Ain't One Thing, It's Another (9 and f)	High Water 1005

Sunset Travelers

Sammy Lee Dortch (lead-1), McKinney Jones (guitar and lead-2), Sylvester Ward (tenor), Grover Blake (baritone), Leon Lumpkin (baritone), Robert Lewis (bass), and Joe Duke (drums)
Houston, Texas, January 20, 1953

ACA2385	Wish I Was in Heaven Sitting Down (1)	Duke 204
ACA2387	I Am Building a Home (1)	Duke 204
ACA2389	My Number Will Be Changed (2)	Duke 201
ACA2390	Yes, Yes, I've Done My Duty (1 and 2)	Duke 201

Memphis, Tennessee, May 16, 1957
O. V. Wright replaces Sammy Lee Dortch and McKinney Jones; Junior Thompson replaces Robert Lewis; add Tommy Tucker (tenor) and Sylvester McKinney (guitar)

Sit Down and Rest a Little While	Pea-Vine PLP 9051

Sources and Resources

This book is largely shaped by interviews and oral histories conducted with quartet singers and other members of the Memphis quartet community. Of secondary importance to these primary sources is the slim corpus of written material related to black American gospel quartets, most of which has been published by Lynn Abbott, Ray Funk, and Doug Seroff. None of these researchers has any academic affiliations or advanced scholarly training in folklore, ethnomusicology, anthropology, or oral history, which is not unusual in the field of American vernacular music. A strong orientation toward historical, biographical, and discographical information places them in the mainstream of writers who have contributed significantly to our knowledge and understanding of blues, rock 'n' roll, and jazz.

These researchers have written largely for popular and "fan" journals such as *Whiskey, Women and . . . , Goldmine,* and *Blues Unlimited,* or brochure notes for long-playing records. Such "amateur" journal articles and "commercial" album productions might discourage the less adventuresome academic scholars from taking their work seriously. However, their publications generally include substantial, groundbreaking research taken from a large body of previously unexplored primary material gleaned from newspaper files, interviews, photographs, college yearbooks, and archives. And their work is finally gaining some of the recognition it deserves. Two of Seroff's brochure notes, "Birmingham Quartet Anthology: Jefferson County, Alabama (1926–1953)" and "The Human Orchestra," were nominated for Grammy Awards in 1982 and 1985, respectively. The most intensive, least recognized single work is Abbott's monograph on New Orleans's Siprocco Singers, published by the National Park Service. Most recently Ray Funk had been annotating and producing a well-received, groundbreaking series of gospel quartet anthologies for an English label, Heritage.

Viv Broughton's 1985 book, *Black Gospel: An Illustrated History of the Gospel Sound,* nicely complements Tony Heilbut's groundbreaking 1971 study, *The Gospel Sound: Good News and Bad Times.* Both offer a popular history of the genre and contain many references and substantial information related to quartets. One major drawback of their work is an obsessive orientation toward the most commercially successful quartets, which badly understates the role of the nonprofessional community groups. Furthermore, neither author footnotes specific references and quotes, an annoying limitation endemic to books aimed at a mass audience.

Three academic writers—George Ricks, Charles Cobb, and Kerill Rubman—have also discussed some aspect of this genre. Ricks's transcription and analyses of several quartet selections appeared in his 1958 dissertation, *Some Aspects of the Religious Music of the United States Negro: An Ethnomusicological Study with Special Emphasis on the Gospel Tradition.* His research is noteworthy for its quality and because it is the first book-length study by a black music scholar to critically examine contemporary Afro-American religious music.

In 1974 Charles Cobb completed a master's thesis in music, "A Theoretical Analysis of Black American Quartet Gospel Music," which notates the harmonic progressions found on commercial recordings of five popular quartets from the 1950s—the Dixie Hummingbirds, the Mighty Clouds of Joy, the Sensational Nightingales, the Soul Stirrers, and the Swan Silvertone Singers. Despite Cobb's excessive thoroughness—nearly 600 pages of analysis are included—his work is of minor importance: his principal conclusion is that the progressions used by these performers are highly repetitive.

Kerill Rubman's 1980 folklore master's thesis, "From 'Jubilee' to 'Gospel' in Black Male Quartet Singing," is a historical survey covering the years 1880 to 1960. Its simultaneous value and limitation lies in the scope of the research, which is almost too broad. But the real strengths of this work are the interviews Rubman conducted with several important quartet singers and her ability to encapsulate large amounts of information.

Even with these publications, a paucity of primary and secondary information haunts this book, particulary in chapter 1. The research available today makes it impossible to construct an accurate, comprehensive historical survey of Afro-American gospel quartets. A massive, complex, and challenging task awaits anyone attempting such a study, though Rubman and Seroff have made a strong start.

A notable lack of primary sources also hampered my research in Memphis and is typified by the information gathered from the local black-oriented newspapers—the *Memphis World* and the *Tri-State Defender.* I examined the available issues of these papers from 1931, when the *Memphis World* began publication, until 1960, the dusk of the quartets' popularity. It was a fruitful yet frustrating search that yielded many minor facts, some program announcements, and a few grainy photographs. I also discovered, much to my astonishment, that no library or archive in the United States owns a complete run of the *Memphis World* and that very few issues from 1931 through 1943 have been preserved. Because the *Tri-State Defender* did not begin its weekly publication until 1951, a critical information gap exists.

The lack of printed sources within the black community's press makes it impossible, for instance, to pinpoint specific information regarding the broadcasting activity of quartets during the 1930s. Radio station logs from this period were disposed of decades ago, and the two daily newspapers, the *Commercial Appeal* and the *Press Scimitar,* did not carry regular radio listings for black groups. For that matter, neither of the white newspapers published very many stories about black religious music.

Nor is the recording activity of local quartets easy to document, particularly in recent years when the groups tended to work with small, Memphis-based companies. Style Wooten's Designer label and the Fernwood Record Company are almost impossible to detail because they are so ephemeral. Such labels issued relatively few discs and operated from as many as three different addresses over a five-year period. None of these companies kept accurate files or logs for their sessions, which means that compiling a comprehensive discography of Memphis quartets is a task that lies somewhere between an inexact science and detective work.

Photographs proved to be one helpful primary source. I located nearly one hundred prints that represent a visual portrait of Memphis's black gospel quartets from 1937 to the present. These photographs came primarily from individuals—most important were those from Mrs. Essie Wade, Cleo Satterfield, Jack Franklin, and Jethroe Bledsoe. Photographs, along with other related paper material such as posters, handbills, and programs, were useful in piecing together the history of Memphis quartets because they provided a visual, tangible link to the past.

But the paramount sources for primary information were still the personal experiences and life stories of the singers, which were supplemented by information gleaned from written sources like the city directory and newspaper accounts. The sources described in this essay underscore the research limitations unique to this study and help to explain how *"Happy in the Service of the Lord"* was shaped and why certain historical, cultural, and discographical facets of quartet singing are not examined as thoroughly as they deserve to be.

Interviews

Except for the interviews with Grover Blake (February 1, 1981), Earl Malone (August 5, 1979), Nathanial Peck (April 28, 1981), Nina Jai Daugherty (May 7 and 12, 1981), and Julia Anderson Todd and Tommie Todd (February 1, 1981), which were conducted by Doug Seroff; with Earl Malone (October 11, 1980), which was conducted by Doug Seroff and Brenda MacCallum; with Jethroe Bledsoe (January 31, 1981), Nathanial Peck (January 31, 1981), and Mary L. Thomas and Doris Jean Gary (February 3, 1983), which were conducted by Doug Seroff and Kip Lornell; and with Jack Miller (June 6, 1979), which was conducted by David Evans, all of the following interviews were conducted by Kip Lornell in Memphis, Tennessee. Transcripts and copies of these taped interviews are deposited at the Mississippi Valley Collection, Brister Library, Memphis State University.

Miller, Frank, August 8, 1982
Miller, Jack, June 6, 1979; February 1980
Moody, Leon, February 8, 1981
Moore, Ernest, May 31, 1982
Moore, Huddie, February 2, 1983
Neal, Willie, April 14, 1981
Nelson, Ford, June 2, 1981
Peck, Nathanial, January 31, 1981; April 28, 1981
Readers, Julius, May 28, 1982
Rodgers, Will, June 9, 1982
Rooks, George, April 27, 1982
Royston, Robert, April 21, 1982
Ruffin, Elijah, March 2, 1981

Satterfield, Cleo, June 7, 1982
Satterfield, Louis, May 29, 1982
Savage, Avery, March 22, 1982
Shells, James, May 5, 1982
Thomas, Mary, February 3, 1983
Todd, Julia and Tommie, February 1, 1981
Todd, Tommie, August 11, 1982
Wade, Theo, October 1979
Walton, Eugene, March 1980; February 2, 1982
Wiley, Floyd, March 15, 1982
Winfield, Harry, July 7, 1982
Wooten, Style, July 17, 1982

Bibliography

Abbott, Lynn. "The New Orleans Humming Four," *Whiskey, Women, and . . . ,* 13 (1984), pp. 4–8.

————. Liner notes, *New Orleans Gospel Quartets 1947–1956,* Heritage HT 306.

————. "The Soproco Spiritual Singers: A New Orleans Quartet Family Tree" (New Orleans: National Park Service, n.d.).

Allen, Raymond. "Old-Time Music and the Urban Folk Revival" (M.A. thesis, Western Kentucky University, 1980).

————. "Old-Time Music and the Urban Folk Revival," *New York Folklore Quarterly,* 7 (1981), pp. 65–81.

————. "'Singing in the Spirit': An Ethnography of Gospel Performance in New York City's African American Church Community" (Ph.D. dissertation, University of Pennsylvania, 1987).

Allen, William, Charles Ware, and Lucy McKim Garrison. *Slaves Songs of the United States.* New York: Oak Publications, 1965 (originally published in 1867).

Bechtol, Paul. "Migration and Economic Opportunities in Tennessee Counties" (Ph.D. dissertation, Vanderbilt University, 1962).

Ben-Amos, Dan. "Towards a Definition of Folklore in Context," *Journal of American Folklore,* 84 (1971), pp. 3–15.

Boyd, Joe Dan. "Judge Jackson: Black Giant of White Spirituals," *Mississippi Folklore Register,* 4 (1970), pp. 7–11.

Boyer, Horace. "Gospel Music," *Music Educators Journal,* 64 (1978), pp. 34–43.

————. "Contemporary Gospel," *The Black Perspective in Music,* 7 (no. 1, 1979), pp. 5–59.

————. "Charles Albert Tindley: Progenitor of Afro-American Gospel Music," *The Black Perspective in Music,* 11 (no. 2, 1981), pp. 103–33.

————. "A Comparative Analysis of Traditional and Contemporary Gospel Music," in *More Than Dancing: Essays on Afro-American Music and Musicians,* ed. Irene Jackson. Westport, Conn.: Greenwood Press, 1985, pp. 127–47.

Bremer, Frederika. *The Homes of the New World: Impressions of America.* New York: Harper and Brothers, 1853. Quoted in Dena Epstein, *Sinful Tunes and Spirituals.* Urbana: University of Illinois Press, 1977, p. 164.

Broughton, Viv. *Black Gospel: An Illustrated History of the Gospel Sound.* Dorset, England: Blandford Press, 1985.

Burnim, Mellonee. "The Black Gospel Music Tradition: A Complex of Ideology, Aesthetic, and Behavior," in *More Than Dancing: Essays on Afro-American Music and Musicians,* ed. Irene Jackson. Westport, Conn.: Greenwood Press, 1985, pp. 148–69.

Byrd, Walter. "The Shape-Note Singing Convention as a Musical Institution in Alabama" (M.A. thesis, University of Alabama, 1962).

Carney, George O. "Geography of Music: A Bibliography," *Journal of Cultural Geography,* 1 (1981), pp. 185–86.

Cobb, Charles. "A Theoretical Analysis of Black American Quartet Gospel Music" (M.A. thesis, University of Wisconsin, 1974).

Courlander, Harold. *Negro Music U.S.A.* New York: Columbia University Press, 1963.

Davis, George, and Fred Donaldson. *Blacks in the United States: A Geographic Perspective.* Boston: Houghton Mifflin, 1975.

Davis, Hank. "Sun's Jones Brothers," *Whiskey, Women, and . . . ,* no. 16 (Spring 1987), pp. 16, 17.

Densmore, Frances. *Chippewa Music.* Washington, D.C.: Smithsonian Institution, 1910.

————. *Nootka and Quileute Music.* Washington, D.C.: Smithsonian Institution, 1939.

Dorson, Richard. *Folklore and Folklife.* Chicago: University of Chicago Press, 1972.

Dyen, Doris. "The Role of Black Shape-Note Music in the Musical Culture of Black Communities in Southeast Alabama" (Ph.D. dissertation, University of Illinois, 1977).

Escott, Colin, and Martin Hawkins. *Sun Records: The Brief History of the Legendary Record Label.* New York: Quick Fox, 1980.

Evans, David. "The Roots of Afro-American Gospel Music," *Jazzforschung,* 8 (1976), pp. 119–35.

————. *Big Road Blues: Tradition and Creativity in the Folk Blues.* Berkeley: University of California Press, 1982.

————. Liner notes, *Let's Get Loose,* New World Records NW 290.

Feintuck, Burt. "A Noncommercial Black Gospel Group in Context: We Live the Life We Sing About," *Black Music Research Journal,* 1 (1980), pp. 37–50.

Ferris, William. *Blues from the Delta.* New York: Doubleday, 1979.

Foreman, Ronald. "Jazz and Race Records, 1920–1932" (Ph.D. dissertation, University of Illinois, 1968).

Foster, George. "What Is Folk Culture?" *American Anthropologist,* 55 (1953), pp. 159–73.

Funk, Ray. "The Imperial Quintet," *Blues and Rhythm—The Gospel Truth,* 9 (1985), pp. 4, 5.

————. Liner notes, *Atlanta Gospel,* Heritage HT 312.

————. Liner notes, *Detroit Gospel,* Heritage HT 311.

————. Liner notes, *Norfolk Jubilee Quartet 1927/1938,* Heritage HT 310.

Gardner, Judith, and Richard McMann. "Culture, Community, and Identity: Working Definition," in *Culture, Community, and Identity,* ed. Judith Garner and Richard McMann. Detroit: Wayne State University Press, 1976, pp. 11–12.

Godrich, John, and Robert M. W. Dixon. *Blues and Gospel Records 1902–1943,* 3d ed. Essex, England: Storyville Publications, 1982.

Grendysa, Pete. "The Golden Gate Quartet," *Record Exchanger,* 5 (1976), pp. 5–9.

————. "Lee Gaines—Singing Low for the Delta Rhythm Boys," *Goldmine,* March 1979, pp. 10–23.

————. "Harry Douglas and the Deep River Boys," *Goldmine,* July 1979, pp. 6–11.

Heilbut, Tony. *The Gospel Sound: Good News and Bad Times,* 2d ed. New York: Simon and Schuster, 1985.

Herzog, George. "The Yuman Music Style," *Journal of American Folklore,* 41 (1928), pp. 183–231.

Hood, Mantle. *The Ethnomusicologist,* 2d ed. Kent, Ohio: Kent State University Press, 1984.

Jackson, Irene. *Afro-American Religious Music: A Bibliography and a Catalogue of Gospel Music.* Westport, Conn.: Greenwood Press, 1979.

Johnson, James Weldon. "The Origins of the 'Barber Chord'," *The Mentor,* February 1929, p. 53.

Jones, A. M. *Studies in African Music.* London: Oxford University Press, 1959.

Kubik, Gerhard. *The Kachamba Brothers Band: A Study of Neo-Traditional Music in Malawi.* Manchester, England: University of Manchester Press, 1974.

Levine, Lawrence. *Black Culture and Black Consciousness.* New York: Oxford University Press, 1977.

Lomax, Alan. *Folk Song Style and Culture.* Washington, D.C.: American Association for the Advancement of Science, 1968.

———. *Cantometrics.* Berkeley: University of California Press, 1976.

Lornell, Kip. "Afro-American Gospel Quartets: An Annotated Bibliography and LP Discography of Pre-War Recordings," *John Edwards Memorial Foundation Quarterly,* 61 (1981), pp. 19–24.

———. "The Geography of American Music: Diffusion, Migration, and Sense of Place," *Current Musicology,* 37/8 (1984), pp. 127–35.

———. "Spatial Perspectives on the Field Recording of Traditional American Music: A Case Study from Tennessee in 1928," in *The Sounds of People and Places: Readings in the Geography of American Folk and Popular Music,* ed. George Carney. Washington, D.C.: University Press of America, 1987, pp. 91–101.

———. "Black Folk Music in Piedmont North Carolina," in *North Carolina Folklore Reader,* ed. Daniel Patterson and Terry Zug (unpublished manuscript).

———. Brochure notes, *Tidewater Blues,* Blue Ridge Institute Records BRI 006, p. 6.

———. Brochure notes, *Happy in the Service of the Lord: Memphis Quartet Heritage—The 1980s,* High Water Records 1002.

Lovell, John. *Black Song: The Forge and the Flame.* New York: Macmillan, 1972.

McCallum, Brenda, and Ray Funk. Brochure notes, *Birmingham Boys— Jubilee Quartets from Jefferson County, Alabama,* Alabama Traditions. LP 101.

Marsh, J. B. T. *The Story of the Jubilee Singers.* Cleveland: Cleveland Printing and Publishing, n.d.

Martin, Deac. "The Evolution of Barbershop Harmony," *Music Journal Annual,* 23 (1965), pp. 24, 106.

———. *Book of Musical America.* New York: Prentice-Hall, 1970.

Martinsdale, Donald. *Social Life and Cultural Change.* New York: Van Nostrand, 1962.

Maultsby, Portia. "Afro-American Religious Music: A Study in Musical Diversity" (Wittenberg, Ohio: Hymn Society of America, 1979).

———. Review of *Jubilee to Gospel: A Selection of Commercially Recorded Black Religious Music, 1921–1953,* JEMF-108, in *Ethnomusicology,* 27 (1983), pp. 162–63.

Merriam, Alan. "African Music," in *Continuity and Change in African Cultures,* ed. William Bascom and Melville Herskovits. Chicago: University of Chicago Press, 1959, pp. 49–86.

———. *The Anthropology of Music.* Evanston: Northwestern University Press, 1966.

Merriam, Alan, and Raymond Mack. "The Jazz Community," *Social Forces,* 38 (1960), pp. 200–219.

Moonoogian, George, and Roger Meeden. "Duke Records—The Early Years: An Interview with David J. Mattis," *Whiskey, Women, and. . . ,* 14 (June 1983), pp. 14–18.

Nettl, Bruno. *Theory and Method in Ethnomusicology.* New York: Free Press of Glencoe, 1963.

Oliver, Paul. *Story of the Blues.* Philadelphia: Chilton Book, 1969.

———. "Black Gospel Music," in *New Grove Dictionary of Music and Musicians,* vol. 7, ed. Stanley Sadie. London: Macmillan, 1980, pp. 254–59.

Raichelson, Richard. "Black Religious Folksong: A Study in Generic and Social Change" (Ph.D. dissertation, University of Pennsylvania, 1975).

Redd, Lawrence. *Rock Is Rhythm and Blues.* East Lansing: Michigan State University Press, 1974.

Ricks, George. *Some Aspects of the Religious Music of the United States Negro: An Ethnomusicological Study with Special Emphasis on the Gospel Tradition.* New York: Arno Press, 1970.

Riis, Thomas. "Black Musical Theater in New York, 1890–1915" (Ph.D. dissertation, University of Michigan, 1981).

Roberts, Helen. *Musical Areas in Aboriginal North America.* New Haven: Yale University Publications in Anthropology, 1936.

Rubman, Kerill. "From 'Jubilee' to 'Gospel' in Black Male Quartet Singing" (M.A. thesis, University of North Carolina, 1980).

Rust, Brian. *Jazz Records 1897–1942.* New Rochelle, N.Y.: Arlington House, 1978.

Sachs, Curt. *Geist und Werden der Musikinstrumente.* Berlin: J. Ard, 1929.

Schaefer, William, and Johannes Reidel. *The Art of Ragtime.* Baton Rouge: Louisiana State University Press, 1973.

Seroff, Douglas. "Sing Me That Song Again: An Interview with Lewis Herring," *Blues Unlimited,* 139 (1980), pp. 24–26.

———. "Polk Miller and the Old South Quartette," *John Edwards Memorial Foundation Quarterly,* 18 (1982), pp. 147–50.

———. "On the Battlefield," in *Repercussions,* ed. Geoffrey Haydon and Dennis Marks. London: Century Publishing, 1985, pp. 30–54.

————. Brochure notes, *"Bless My Bones": Memphis Gospel Radio—The 1950s,* Pea-Vine PLP 9051.

Simond, Ike. *Old Slack's Reminiscences and Pocket History of the Colored Profession from 1865 to 1891.* Chicago: by the author, 1891.

Southern, Eileen. "W. Herbert Brewster," in *Biographical Dictionary of Afro-American and African Music.* Westport, Conn.: Greenwood Press, 1982, p. 47.

————. "Lucie Eddie Campbell," in *Biographical Dictionary of Afro-American and African Music.* Westport, Conn.: Greenwood Press, 1982, p. 51.

————. *The Music of Black America,* 2d ed. New York: W. W. Norton, 1983.

Stebbins, Robert. "The Jazz Community: The Sociology of a Musical Sub-Culture" (Ph.D. dissertation, University of Minnesota, 1964).

————. "A Theory of the Jazz Community," in *American Music: From Storyville to Woodstock.* ed. Charles Nanry. New Brunswick, N.J.: Transactional Books, 1972, pp. 115–34.

Tallmadge, William. Brochure notes, *Jubilee to Gospel: A Selection of Commercially Recorded Black Religious Music 1921–1953,* JEMF-108.

Titon, Jeff. *Early Downhome Blues: A Musical and Cultural Analysis.* Urbana: University of Illinois Press, 1977.

————. *Downhome Blues Lyrics.* Boston: G. K. Hall, 1982.

Toll, Robert. *Blacking Up: The Minstrel Show in Nineteenth-Century America.* New York: Oxford University Press, 1974.

Walker, Wyatt Tee. *"Somebody's Calling My Name": Black Sacred Music and Social Change.* Valley Forge, Pa.: Judson Press, 1979.

Wittke, Carl. *Tambo and Bones.* Durham, N.C.: Duke University Press, 1930.

Work, John. "Plantation Meistersinger," *Musical Quarterly,* 39 (1941), pp. 41–49.

Index

A Note on the Author

Kip Lornell is a staff folklorist with the Blue Ridge Institute of Ferrum College, Ferrum, Virginia. He has a master's degree in folklore from the University of North Carolina–Chapel Hill and a doctorate in ethnomusicology from Memphis State University. The author of over fifty articles for popular and scholarly music and folklore publications, Lornell has also written *Virginia's Blues, Country, and Gospel Records, 1902–43: An Annotated Discography.*

Books in the Series Music in American Life

Only a Miner: Studies in Recorded Coal-Mining Songs
Archie Green

Great Day Coming: Folk Music and the American Left
Serge Denisoff

John Philip Sousa: A Descriptive Catalog of His Works
Paul E. Bierley

The Hell-Bound Train: A Cowboy Songbook
Glenn Ohrlin

Oh, Didn't He Ramble: The Life Story of Lee Collins
as Told to Mary Collins
Frank J. Gillis and John W. Miner, Editors

American Labor Songs of the Nineteenth Century
Philip S. Foner

Stars of Country Music: Uncle Dave Macon
to Johnny Rodriguez
Bill C. Malone and Judith McCulloh, Editors

Git Along, Little Dogies: Songs and Songmakers
of the American West
John I. White

Texas-Mexican *Cancionero:* Folksongs of
the Lower Border
Americo Paredes

San Antonio Rose: The Life and Music of Bob Wills
Charles R. Townsend

Early Downhome Blues: A Musical and Cultural Analysis
Jeff Todd Titon

An Ives Celebration: Papers and Panels of the Charles Ives
Centennial Festival-Conference
Wiley Hitchcock and Vivian Perlis, Editors

Sinful Tunes and Spirituals: Black Folk Music
to the Civil War
Dena J. Epstein

Joe Scott, the Woodsman-Songmaker
Edward D. Ives

Jimmie Rodgers: The Life and Times of America's
Blue Yodeler
Nolan Porterfield

Early American Music Engraving and Printing: A History
of Music Publishing in America from 1787 to 1825
with Commentary on Earlier and Later Practices
Richard J. Wolfe

Sing a Sad Song: The Life of Hank Williams
Roger M. Williams

Long Steel Rail: The Railroad in American Folksong
Norm Cohen

Resources of American Music History: A Directory of Source
Materials from Colonial Times to World War II
D. W. Krummel, Jean Geil, Doris J. Dyen, and Deane L. Root

Tenement Songs: The Popular Music of the Jewish Immigrants
Mark Slobin

Ozark Folksongs
Vance Randolph; Edited and Abridged by Norm Cohen

Oscar Sonneck and American Music
William Lichtenwanger, Editor

Bluegrass Breakdown: The Making of the Old Southern Sound
Robert Cantwell

Bluegrass: A History
Neil V. Rosenberg

Music at the White House: A History of the American Spirit
Elise K. Kirk

Red River Blues: The Blues Tradition in the Southeast
Bruce Bastin

Good Friends and Bad Enemies: Robert Winslow Gordon
and the Study of American Folksong
Debora Kodish

Fiddlin' Georgia Crazy: Fiddlin' John Carson, His Real World,
and the World of His Songs
Gene Wiggins

America's Music: From the Pilgrims to the Present
Revised Third Edition
Gilbert Chase

Secular Music in Colonial Annapolis: The Tuesday Club, 1745–56
John Barry Talley

Bibliographical Handbook of American Music
D. W. Krummel

Goin' to Kansas City
Nathan W. Pearson, Jr.